THE ESSENTIAL GUIDE FOR VOTING

The Case For Voting Democratic
North Carolina
2024

Compiled and Written by

Jim Porto
Voter, Townhall Precinct
Orange County, NC

Savvylion Press

ISBN: 978-1-7341536-0-6
Title: The Essential Guide for Voting
Series: Essential Guides for State Voting
State Edition: North Carolina

Front cover image by James V Porto
Book design by James V Porto

Printed in the United States of America

1st Edition 2024

SavvyLion Press, an Imprint from SavvyLion Learning, LLC
107 Watters Rd
Carrboro, NC 27510-1323

Don't interfere with anything in the Constitution. That must be maintained, for it is the only safeguard of our liberties. ABRAHAM LINCOLN

The Constitution is the sole source and guaranty of national freedom. CALVIN COOLIDGE

Most faults are not in our Constitution, but in ourselves. RAMSEY CLARK

Our constitution works. Our great republic is a government of laws, not of men. GERALD FORD

I am persuaded there is among the mass of our people a fund of wisdom, integrity, and humanity which will preserve their happiness in a tolerable measure. JOHN ADAMS

Anyone who has ever lived under a dictatorship which cannot be removed without bloodshed will know that democracy, imperfect though it is, is worth fighting for and, I believe, worth dying for. SIR KARL POPPER

There are similarities between absolute power and absolute faith: a demand for absolute obedience, a readiness to attempt the impossible, a bias for simple solutions—to cut the knot rather than unravel it, the viewing of compromise as surrender. Both absolute power and absolute faith are instruments of dehumanization. Hence, absolute faith corrupts as absolutely as absolute power. ERIC HOFFER

The root of all evil is the abuse of power. JIM PORTO

We (Nazis) enter Parliament in order to supply ourselves, in the arsenal of democracy, with its own weapons. If democracy is so stupid as to give us free tickets and salaries for this bear's work, that is its affair. JOSEPH GOEBBELS

I believe that leaders must display dignity. I believe that leaders must tell the truth. I believe that leaders should be able to laugh at themselves. I believe leaders must care for and love the people they are leading. I believe leaders must possess knowledge and expertise, but with full awareness that none of us has all the answers. With Kamala Harris and Tim Walz, I see all those qualities. STEPH CURRY

CRITICAL DATES FOR THE 2024 ELECTION CYCLE

Sept 6, 2024: County Board of Elections begins mailing absentee ballots.

Oct. 11, 2024 (5:00pm): Mail-in Registration most be postmarked no later than 25 days before election which is Oct 11, 2024. If the County Board of Elections does not receive the registration within 5 days of the postmark, it will be processed after the election. The unregistered voter may still register to vote in person during the early voting period.

Oct 17, 2024 through Nov 2, 2024 (3:00pm): Early Voting Period.

Oct 29, 2024 (5:00pm): Absentee ballot request deadline.

Nov 5, 2024 (6:30am to 7:30pm): Election Day.

Nov 5, 2024 (7:30pm): Deadline to return absentee ballot. IMPORTANT: Absentee ballots must be RECEIVED by the county Board of Elections by this time. A postmark date no longer counts.

Nov, 15 2024: Statewide canvas to determine provisional votes. Provisional voters should return all information well before this deadline to clear their ballots.

OFFICES UP FOR ELECTION IN THE 2024 ELECTION CYCLE

U.S. President/Vice President
U.S. House of Representatives
Governor
Lieutenant Governor
Secretary of State
State Auditor
State Treasurer
Superintendent of Public Instruction
Attorney General
Agriculture Commissioner
Labor Commissioner
Insurance Commissioner
State Senator
State Representative
N.C. Supreme Court Justice
N.C. Court of Appeals Judge
Superior Court Judge
District Court Judge
District Attorney
County Commissioner
Clerk of Superior Court
Register of Deeds

Many counties have elections for boards of commissioners and boards of education. A number of municipalities also have elections for mayor and seats on the municipal governing board.

Contents

PREFACE

Upon leaving the final session of the Constitutional Convention of 1787, Benjamin Franklin was asked: "Well, Doctor, what have we got, a republic or a monarchy?" Franklin is said to have replied, "A republic, Madam, if you can keep it."

The United States is the oldest surviving democracy, and one of the few that has lasted more than 200 years. The ancient Greeks thought democracies were inherently unstable and would always fall to the strong man, often a charismatic tyrant masquerading as a leader "of the people."

The founding fathers were well aware of the dangers of demagogues and enshrined the US Constitution in a written document, the first of its kind, with features meant to preserve the rule of law so that it would be harder for a would-be tyrant to take power.

Every generation has seen challenges to the American democracy and has been called upon to defend it for future generations. Our time has come. We are facing the gravest threat since World War II. This time the threat is from within by a subversive group that has been cultivated by our greatest adversary. This threat needs to be thoroughly trounced at the voting booth.

Join the **Pro-Democracy Coalition** to defeat MAGA authoritarians and Christian Nationalists (should their brand of Christianity be called *Christian-ism*?) who are designing a Trumpian Christian Nationalist dictatorship. Let's not make the same mistakes the German people did in 1933 that gave power to Hitler.

This voting guide was originally written for Orange County, NC, but most of the content is applicable throughout the state. All county specific information can be found at county websites. Orange County data may be viewed as examples of what is available to all counties in NC.

Our intent is to distribute this document to as many citizens as possible. If citizens of other jurisdictions are interested in seeing more state guides developed tailored to their states, contact the author.

This is a compiled document mostly from sources that are publically available. I have provided links to these sources. For much of Chapter four I have used exact instructions or descriptions given at these sites because these are authoritative sources.

For those sources that are not governmental, typically not-for-profit (org) sites, I have included in-line references to them. In some cases I used ChatGPT 4.0 to identify key points, which I re-worded and added details to be more informative. In other cases, I wrote the paragraphs based upon my understanding and beliefs about what is happening now.

The quotations used in this booklet come from *Power Quotes* by Daniel B. Baker, Visible Ink Press, 1992, except for two I interjected.

The photographs of Women and Men at War on the last page are from the National Archives.

If any source feels as if I have not given proper attribution, please notify me and I will make the change. Information in this document is meant to be shared as a form of common wisdom about American democracy and the threats from authoritarian efforts to undermine it.

Table 0.1: QRCodes

James (Jim) V Porto
Editor
SavvyLion Press

Reader

The Deplorables

WHY VOTE: A SHORT LIST

1. Are you working at a minimum wage job? Republicans oppose a twenty dollar per hour minimum wage. Democrats support it.

2. Are you a student burdened with student loans? Republicans oppose loan forgiveness. Democrats support loan forgiveness.

3. Are you a working parent and have few options for childcare? Republicans refuse to fund affordable childcare. Democrats support funding affordable childcare.

4. Are you, a parent, or a grandparent who depends on Social Security? Republicans want to cut Social Security. Democrats want to enhance Social Security.

5. Do you have a friend or relative who is gay? Republicans want to deny rights to the LGBTQ community and to stigmatize them and their friends. Democrats support gay rights.

6. Do you know of anyone who has had an unintended or problematic pregnancy? Republicans want to outlaw abortion, even if the woman has been raped or is a victim of incest! Democrats support the right for women to choose.

7. Do you think Climate Change is real, and we need to act to reverse the change? Republicans think Climate Change is a hoax and want to deny funding to address it. Democrats are funding actions to stop climate change.

8. Have you or a friend ever committed a minor infraction and had to account for your actions? Republicans think that if they have money and power they are above the law. They believe the rule of law does not apply to the wealthy and powerful. Democrats believe no one is above the law, even presidents.

9. Do you have a friend or family member who served in the Marines, Army, Navy, Air Force, Coast Guard or National Guard? Republicans want to cut funding to the VA and have become hostile and disrespectful to our military. Democrats support funding of the VA and other military assistance programs.

10. Do you, a family member, or a friend depend on Obamacare, Medicare, or Medicaid? The Republicans want to decrease fund-

ing to public health insurance programs. Democrats passed Obamacare with no help from the Republicans.

11. Do you think it should be easy to vote in a democracy? Republicans are afraid of losing and are making it hard for working-class citizens, the elderly, the disabled, and minorities to vote. Democrats are working to protect voting rights.

12. Do you think that the genius of our founding fathers was to set up checks and balances within the government so no one person can gain too much power? Republicans are planning to strip all checks and balances and concentrate power in the Presidency if they win. Democrats are against dictatorships.

13. Only by voting for Democratic candidates will these issues be addressed.

WARNING: A VOTE FOR REPUBLICANS IS A VOTE TO CUT SOCIAL SECURITY.

############

The ballot is stronger than the bullet. ABRAHAM LINCOLN

We'd all like to vote for the best man, but he's never a candidate. KIN HUBBARD

Voting is a civic sacrament. THEODORE HESBURGH

An election is a bet on the future, not a popularity test of the past. JAMES RESTON

Bad politicians are sent to Washington by good people who don't vote. WILLIAM SIMON

Inside the polling booth every American man and woman stands as the equal of every other American man and woman. There they have no superiors. There they have no masters save their own minds and consciences. FRANKLIN ROOSEVELT

* * *

WHY WE VOTE: A BRIEF HISTORY

The Founding of the Country

In 1774 the US was composed of 13 colonies, each with governing bodies. These colonies were distinct in their populations, economies and social customs. All were ruled by Great Britain under King George III. The abuse of power and disregard of the rule of law when dealing with the colonies brought the colonies together in 1774 to form the First Continental Congress.

Delegates convened in Philadelphia to discuss a unified response to their grievances. They adopted a petition for colonial rights and sent it to King George. Although the King could ignore the petition, he could not ignore the call to boycott all British goods, which the delegates had also imposed. The King dispatched troops to the colonies to break the boycott. This only inflamed tensions and led the colonies to respond.

The Second Continental Congress convened in 1775 to prepare for armed conflict. They appointed George Washington as Commander and raised an army to fight the British. In 1776 the Second Continental Congress issued the Declaration of Independence, laying out the grievances of colonies and justifications for independence.

The revolutionary war lasted eight years and ended in recognition of American independence with the signing of the Treaty of Paris in 1783. During this eight-year struggle, the Second Continental Congress continued to meet and manage the war. Its efforts led to the first governmental structure for the 13 colonies—the Articles of Confederation, which were adopted by the Second Continental Congress in 1777.

The Confederation lasted eleven years to 1788 when the US Constitution, formulated at the Federal Convention of 1787 in Philadelphia, was adopted after New Hampshire ratified it on June 21, 1788.

The major failure of the Confederation was that it had a weak central government. That made it impossible to institute unified policies to address economic, military, law enforcement and diplomatic efforts that protected and advanced interests of the colonies as a whole.

The unity achieved to adopt the Constitution is recognized on the Great Seal of the United States by the Latin phrase "E Pluribus Unum," or "From Many, One."

The colonies declared independence because they were subject to an abusive, authoritarian regime that did not follow the rule of law but carried out decrees on the whims of its tyrant. Adherence to the rule of law and not being subject to the will of a single individual, above all else, are the core principles of the American foundation.

The Intent of the Founding Fathers

The founding fathers were students of history and knew that all governments eventually were seized by ruthless authoritarians who acquired power in one of two ways: office-holding and office transition.

After appointment or election to a powerful executive position, tyrants use institutional offices to concentrate enough power into their hands to seize all power. During transitions after the death of leaders, conditions are ripe for hijacking the regime. Who ascends to power upon the death of a ruler is known as the succession problem.

An innovation of the US Constitution was that checks and balances, primarily on the Executive (but also on the legislative body's natural inclination to become a "tyranny of the majority") were built into the institutional responsibilities of governing elements. Since royal succession had been ruled out by the democratic regime selected by the founders, succession was a problem because it required a system for selecting a ruler, which meant balancing many competing political interests. Office holders had to be either voted into office or appointed by those voted into office. Constructing a succession procedure generated the most controversy at the Federal Convention and necessitated key compromises.

Two questions any designer of a new regime must ask is "who rules? And for whom do they rule?" Direct democracy is the form of regime in which citizens rule, theoretically for the good of all citizens, by voting their preferences on matters of state. But in ancient times, direct democracies had two major problems: a permanent majority could arise and abuse its power by not seeing to the welfare of the voting minority; and direct democracies were vulnerable to demagogues, who were artful at manipulating the votes of citizens through their speaking skills. All ancient democracies failed from one, or both, of these causes.

The ancient philosopher Aristotle believed that a large middle class of artisans would stabilize a regime, thus countering its self-destructive tendencies. But the founders knew that a large middle class was not sufficient to prevent either a tyranny of the majority or the rise of a demagogue.

The solution the founders settled on, and another important innovation in the Constitution, was to design a Representative Democracy in which the will of the people was filtered through agents selected by the people in apportioned districts to represent their interests. These agents were to be selected based on their character, wisdom and willingness to serve all voters, even the minority. And when a demagogue did arise in one of the districts and was selected, his or her impact would be minimal on the whole regime.

The founders also knew that, despite all these measures, there was no guarantee that the American polity would remain a democracy. In particular, the transition from one administration to another required the loser accept the loss and not try to agitate against the newly elected administration.

Even the best designed regime requires a good faith commitment to the process. Would-be tyrants do not accept their defeat and attack the credibility of the process and its institutions. The most effective way to attack legitimate regimes is to repeatedly tell lies about those who won. This method employs the cognitive bias called the Illusion of Truth. The more frequently people hear a lie, the more likely they are to accept it as true even when there is ample evidence contradicting it. All past tyrants used this technique, including Hitler who was a master at it.

The founders designed a representative democracy and recorded it in written form, thereby creating the first Constitutional Democracy in which the procedures and rules necessary for running a representative democracy are clearly laid out. In a Constitutional Democracy, loyalty is given to the Constitution, not to an individual. This allegiance is recognized in the constitutional oath. Everyone joining the military or elected (and appointed) to any federal or state positions swears an oath to the Constitution. (See Appendix III).

Compromises in the Constitution

One of the most distinctive features of the American Polity is that it was designed and not inherited. During any design process with more than one participant, compromise is necessary to obtain agreement on the final draft. Designing a polity requires the political art of compromise, which is available only if all parties are acting in good faith.

Compromise is the best way to ensure stability and consent on decisions. The goal of any polity is to achieve both wisdom and consent on its actions. To reach agreement on the form of government we have, the founders agreed to six compromises that still effect our political life today.

1. *The Great Compromise.* Having decided on a representative democracy rather than a direct democracy, the biggest problem was deciding how to apportion the representatives in the legislative branch. If the apportionment was by population, then the less populous states felt their interests would be ignored by the majority. If the apportionment was by state, the more populous states felt that the less populous (and mostly rural) states would dominate. The compromise was to create a two-chamber legislature. The House of Representatives would be based on population (satisfying the larger states), and the Senate would have equal representation with two senators from each state (addressing the concerns of smaller states).

2. *The Commerce Compromise.* With the recent failure of the Articles of Confederation in mind, especially around a weak central government to regulate trade and make agreements for the colonies, the Founders wanted to ensure the colonies could speak with a unified voice. Many states however wanted to retain trade regulation. The compromise was to grant Congress the power to regulate foreign and interstate commerce while leaving intrastate commerce in the hands of the states.

3. *The Electoral College.* How to select a President presented a problem. Some advocated for direct election from the entire population, which had two problems: (1) it gave the advantage to the most populous states in selecting the president, (2) a demagogue

could more easily capture the presidency. Smaller states wanted their interests expressed in selecting a president. The compromise was that each state would appoint electors equal to its total congressional representation (Senators plus Representatives), who would then vote for the President. Since the Senate was equally apportioned to the states, the resulting college was a reflection of the Great Compromise which gave smaller states more power. Electors were to be discerning enough not to fall under the sway of a demagogue, thus increasing the chances of a good selection to lead the country.

4. *The Supremacy Clause.* The major reason for the Federalists Convention was the federated body provided by the Articles of Confederation did not have a strong central authority. Still, some states did not want to cede too much authority to a central power. The compromise was the Supremacy Clause that established federal authority for all laws passed by Congress, treaties, and the Constitution as the supreme law of the land, binding on all states. States could enact state laws that did not conflict with federal laws.

The following two compromises show that slavery was an issue from the founding of the country.

5. The Southern states wanted to count slaves for representation in the House of Representatives, even though they were not given the vote. The solution was the *Three-Fifths Compromise* in which slaves were counted as three-fifths of a person for determining representation AND taxation.

6. The Northern states wanted to abolish the international slave trade, but the Southern states did not. The *Slave Trade Compromise* allowed Congress to prohibit the importation of enslaved individuals after 1808.

This crack in the Constitution expanded to the breaking point when Abraham Lincoln, an avid opponent of slavery, was elected president 73 years after adoption of the Constitution. With the assault on the federal base at Fort Sumter, S.C. in 1861 the nation entered the darkest chapter in its history. It took a Civil War to abolish slavery and decades of reconstruction to repair the Constitution.

The Bill of Rights

The Constitutional Convention required 9 of the 13 states to ratify the Constitution before it could become the law of the colonies. Even after the compromises above, many states wanted assurances that the central government would not abuse its newly granted authorities and wanted the Constitution to incorporate explicit protections for individual liberties.

James Madison offered the first 10 amendments to the Constitution after ratification to satisfy these requirements. These amendments, which became known as the Bill of Rights, were ratified by the states in 1791.

1. The First Amendment protects freedom of religion, speech, the press, assembly and the right to petition the government.

2. The Second Amendment protects the right to keep and bear arms.

3. The Third Amendment prohibits the forced quartering of soldiers in private homes during peacetime without the owner's consent.

4. The Fourth Amendment protects against unreasonable searches and seizures and requires warrants issued base on probable cause.

5. The Fifth Amendment includes individual protections such as the right to a grand jury, protection against double jeopardy, the right against self-discrimination, due process of law, and protection of private property from government appropriation without just compensation.

6. The Sixth Amendment guarantees the right to a fair and speedy trial, including the right to a jury trial, the right to confront witnesses, and the right to counsel.

7. The Seventh Amendment ensures the right to a jury trial in certain civil cases.

8. The Eighth Amendment prohibits excessive bail and fines, as well as cruel and unusual punishment.

9. The Ninth Amendment affirms that the enumeration of certain rights in the Constitution shall not be construed to deny or disparage others retained by the people.

10. The Tenth Amendment affirms that the powers not delegated to the federal government by the Constitution, nor prohibited to the states, are reserved to the states or to the people.

Since the Bill of rights was adopted, the Constitution has been amended 17 times. The Constitution and the full list amendments are in Appendix I.

The Institutions of Government

The US regime has three branches of government: The legislature (Congress) composed of two chambers (The Great Compromise)—the Senate and the House of Representatives—that make laws, an Executive branch that carries out laws, and a Judicial branch that resolves conflicts around laws.

This design shows the razor-like focus of the founders on the need for rules of law, rather than the whims of a monarchy, as the guiding principle for governing. Each of these branches has powers to carry out their functions and, importantly, to check the powers of the other branches so that they do not accumulate too much power.

Powers and Functions of the Branches of Government

The United States government is founded on the principle of federalism, with powers apportioned to three branches to ensure a balance of power. This system of checks and balances is designed to enable each branch to counterbalance the others, creating a stable and fair governance structure. Below is an overview of the powers, functions, and checks of Congress, the Presidency, and the Supreme Court.

Congress

Legislative Powers. Congress, which consists of two chambers—the House of Representatives and the Senate—holds the power to make laws. It can introduce and pass legislation, levy taxes, declare war, and regulate interstate and foreign commerce.

Budgetary Powers. Congress controls the national purse. It has the authority to draft and pass the budget, and to allocate funds to various government departments and programs. A key feature adopted upon the insistence of larger states, was that only the House could initiate spending measures.

Impeachment Powers. The House of Representatives has the power to impeach federal officials, including the President, for "treason, bribery, or other high crimes and misdemeanors," while the Senate conducts the impeachment trial and has the power to convict and remove officials from office.

Checks on Presidency. Congress can override a presidential veto with a two-thirds majority vote in both the House and the Senate. It also has the power to approve or reject presidential appointments and treaties. Congress can impeach the President for treason or other crimes.

Checks on Supreme Court. Congress can propose constitutional amendments to override judicial decisions, set jurisdictional limits on the Supreme Court including the size of the court, and establish lower courts.

Presidency

Executive Powers. The President is responsible for enforcing and administering federal laws and policies, and serves as head of the executive branch of the federal government.

Military Powers. The President serves as the Commander-in-Chief of the armed forces, with the authority to direct military operations and deploy troops (though Congress holds the power to declare war).

Diplomatic Powers. The President has the power to negotiate and sign treaties (with the Senate's consent), recognize foreign nations, and appoint ambassadors.

Appointment Powers. The President can appoint federal officials, including judges to the federal judiciary (subject to Senate confirmation), and has the power to grant pardons and reprieves for federal offenses

Checks on Congress. The President can veto legislation passed by Congress which then requires a two-thirds majority from both the House and Senate to override it. The President can also veto appointments by Congress, which requires a majority vote in both the House and the Senate.

Checks on Supreme Court. The President nominates justices to the Supreme court, which requires approval from the Senate.

Supreme Court

Judicial Powers. The Supreme Court is the highest court in the United States and has the ultimate authority in interpreting the Constitution and federal law. It has the power of judicial review, which allows it to declare laws or executive actions unconstitutional.

Appellate Jurisdiction. The Court hears appeals on a wide range of legal issues shaping federal law, ensuring uniformity in their interpretation.

Checks on Congress. The Supreme Court not only interprets legislation, it can rule legislation unconstitutional and void.

Checks on Presidency. The Supreme Court presides over the impeachment trial. It also can rule on the constitutionality of executive action.

This system of separated powers with checks and balances is designed to ensure no single branch can dominate the government, promoting a balance that helps protect democratic principles and prevent tyranny.

############

We [Supreme Court] do not sit as a super-legislature to weigh the wisdom of legislation. WILLIAM DOUGLAS

As a member of this court, I am not justified in writing my private notions of policy into the Constitution, no matter how deeply I may cherish them or how mischievous I may deem their disregard. FELIX FRANKFURTER

It is not our job to apply laws that have not yet been written. JOHN PAUL STEVENS

The Court is most vulnerable and comes nearest to illegitimacy when it deals with judge-made constitutional law having little or no cognizable roots in the language or design of the Constitution. BYRAN WHITE

All democracies must manage two perversions: the Tyranny of the Majority and the Tyranny of the Minority. JIM PORTO

* * *

11

KEEPING DEMOCRACY

Brief History of Parties (based on Jackson Turner Main)

Even before the Constitution, political interests separated into two groups: the Localists and the Cosmopolitans.

Localists generally wanted less governmental involvement in society. They were most often from rural areas and were "life" educated. They supported lower taxes. Localists had a restricted world view; their community was the primary focus. They typically voted for issues that benefited only their communities.

They wanted paper money and cheap debt. They were Anti-federalists (against the Constitution and for the Articles of Confederation) because they distrusted authority not based in the local community.

The Cosmopolitans generally wanted more governmental involvement in solving the problems of society because so many problems cut across community boundaries. They were often from Urban Areas and were "book" educated.

They supported higher taxes and a strong central authority. Cosmopolitans had an expansive world view that encompassed all the colonies. They often opposed paper money and high inflation. They were Federalists who supported the Constitution.

The core difference between the two groups may be boiled down to the following: Localists valued autonomy and the uniformity of their local communities, and did not believe in luck; Cosmopolitans valued cooperation and the diversity of a larger community, and believed in luck.

Localists believed that a person was solely responsible for his or her condition. If you were poor or unskilled, you did not work hard enough; if you were rich, you were being rewarded for your high character and hard work.

Cosmopolitans believed that one's condition in life was often a matter of luck, who your were born to and where you were born. Another key difference seen today is that Localists emphasized individualism and Cosmopolitans emphasized cooperative action.

Despite these differences, the two groups compromised on a plan for governing the united colonies as a single nation. To keep the plan together required the losers to consent in their loss.

Election losers abided by the outcome of federal elections until 1861 when slave-holding states separated from the Union upon election of Abraham Lincoln. Only a strong and committed response from Lincoln and the Republican Party kept the Union intact.

A stable polity requires views of both Localists and Cosmopolitans. Localists' suspicion of central authority counters the Cosmopolitans' overreaching with central authority. Cosmopolitans embracing diversity and government action counters the Localists' isolation and slow innovation.

The key is to compromise, which is THE art of governing in a democracy. In the 20th and 21st centuries, these two groups were roughly reflected in the two modern groups: Conservatives and Liberals. After the Civil Rights Act of 1964, the Conservatives migrated to the Republican Party and the Liberals to the Democratic Party.

Another group has always been present on the fringes of American political life. We can call this group the "Benedict Arnold" faction because it wants to betray the foundations of the American democratic polity. This group does not compromise. It seeks to set up a dictatorship that benefits only its members. For many years this group was held in check by both the Democratic and the Republican parties. But with the election of Donald Trump in 2016, who embraced this fringe group, the Republican Party was taken over by authoritarians, leaving conservative Republicans without a party.

The best analogy to understand what has happened to America since 2016 is the human immune system. The body contains many types of bacteria both good and bad. The good bacteria help us stay healthy, while the bad are toxic to the body. When the immune system is robust, it keeps the bad bacteria in check. But if the immune system is stressed, it cannot do its job and bad bacteria increase. The result is that the body becomes sick and can die if not treated.

The American "body" politic has become sick. The immune system of a robust two-party system that believes in the rule of law and losers' consent is broken. This has led the Benedict Arnold authoritarian faction to threaten the entire system. The only remedy now is a complete rejection at the polls for any Republican running for an elective office at all levels of government. That is the purpose of this Voting Guide.

Assault on the American Democracy by Authoritarians

Identifying Authoritarians. The founding fathers were concerned that a tyrant could arise in a Constitutional Democracy. Checks and balances, education, and compromises were part of the design in the constitution to prevent the rise of an inflammatory, would-be tyrant to convince people to vote for him or her. The ancient Greeks had a name for these people: demagogues.

To identify demagogues and usurpers to our Constitutional Democracy, we need to be informed by the actions, not the words, of would-be tyrants that indicate their true intent. So like James, the brother of Jesus who preached that faith without action is useless, politicians should be judged by what they do, not what they say.

The following list are actions that every usurper and dictator from Stalin, Hitler, and Mussolini, to Putin, Erdogan, and Orban has used.

- Attacks free press.
- Tells lies constantly.
- Undermines rule of law.
- Develops a cult following.
- Packs institutions with cult followers.
- Seeks to be the sole authority.
- Takes revenge on political and personal enemies.
- Fosters divisions and encourages violence.
- Makes decisions that benefit only himself or herself.
- Laughs at others' misfortunes.
- Says he/she is defending democracy.
- Accuses others of the authoritarian behaviors he/she practices.

The Republican Party that once participated in shared governance under the rule of law has been taken over by the Trumpian MAGA cult, whose purpose is to convert the United States into a dictatorship using many of these tactics.

These are not conjectures or baseless claims. These aims are expressed openly by MAGA leaders, Christian Nationalists, Billionaires like Elon Musk and Authoritarian Right groups in their publications and websites.

"I love you Christians. I'm a Christian. I love you, get out, you gotta get out and vote. In four years, you don't have to vote again, we'll have it fixed so good you're not going to have to vote." DONALD TRUMP, 26 JULY 2024

"Our primary focus is not to get out the vote, it is to make sure they don't cheat. Because we have all the votes we'll need." DONALD TRUMP, AUGUST 2024 IN NORTH CAROLINA

Assault on Women. A hallmark of this effort is an all-out assault on woman and woman's rights. Here are examples of the MAGA agenda for women.

"In 2021, Texas state Rep. Bryan Slaton introduced a bill that would have criminalized abortion as homicide, punishable by death, for women who have abortions. Slaton, who introduced legislation to finish a portion of a Texas-Mexico border wall and name it after Trump, has pledged to reintroduce the abortion bill.

In the same year in Arizona, 10 state representatives introduced a bill to do the same thing. Among the lawmakers sponsoring the Arizona bill were Trump-supporting state Reps. Walt Blackman and Shawnna Bolick. Bolick said she would not have certified Biden's 2020 victory over Trump in Arizona.

In March 2022, Trump supporter and Louisiana state Rep. Danny McCormick introduced a bill that would have subjected Louisiana women to murder charges for having abortions." (Politifact.com). See Table 3.1 for links.

Fortunately, Marc Elias has assembled a team of lawyers who are defending democracy in court and challenging every outrageous anti-democratic bill passed. His effort is called Democracy Docket and is well worth supporting: https://www.democracydocket.com/.

This is only a small sample of the measures hurting women. Indivisible.org has identified 31 efforts by MAGA to diminish woman in America.

1. Denying reproductive rights.
2. Denying pregnancy as a pre-existing condition and allowing employers to deny birth control coverage.
3. Opposing the Violence Against Women Act.
4. Separating families at the border.
5. Promoting actions that widen the gender pay gap.
6. Undermining gender equality in education.
7. Assaulting LGBTQ+ Rights, a key goal in Project 2025.
8. Pushing abstinence-only sex education instead of evidence-based education.
9. Ignoring the disproportional effect of climate change on women worldwide.
10. Rolling back the clock on gender equality through conservative judicial decisions.
11. Passing tax and jobs acts that prevent working women from acquiring liveable wages.
12. Undermining public health agencies that predominantly serve women.
13. Decimating the social safety net.
14. Defending sexual predators, especially political allies, and blaming the victim.
15. Undermining women's health research by opposing funding for women's health issues.
16. Sacrificing international women's rights by reducing funding for women's UN agencies.
17. Worsening the maternal healthcare crisis that predominately impact minority women.
18. Encouraging immigration policies that terrorize women seeking asylum.
19. Obstructing economic justice for women by not supporting minimum wage laws.
20. Mismanaging the pandemic which hit women hardest economically.
21. Refusing to support child care and paid leave.
22. Cutting education support that disproportionately benefit women.
23. Opposing adoption of the Equal Rights Amendment.

24. Reducing global family planning resources.
25. Eroding election integrity, disproportionately affecting women since they vote more than men.
26. Suppressing women's voices in politics as shown by underrepresented elected officials.
27. Dismantling asylum protections for victims of gender-based violence.
28. Undermining pregnancy discrimination protections against unscrupulous employers.
29. Restricting access to safe and affordable housing, especially for single mothers.
30. Dismantled the White House Council on Women and Girls.
31. Mainstreaming misogyny.

Table 3.1: QRCodes

Women as Criminals   Assaults on Women

You can find references to material that document their claims at their website. See Table 3.1.

To read a comprehensive history of the assault on women's rights, see *The Fall of Roe: The Rise of a New America* by Elizabeth Dias and Lisa Lerer. Table 3.2 has the book URL.

The compelling question for MAGA men, and most are MAGA men who push these efforts, is: Why are you doing this?

Christian Nationalism. The answer is that a perverted form of Christianity, contrary to Jesus's message, called Christian Nationalism advocates the subjugation of women. This perversion of Christianity has infil-

Table 3.2: QRCodes

The Fall Of Roe

Rise of Christian Nationalism

trated the MAGA cult and seeks to dominate every level of American society.

"The goal [of Christian Nationalism] is not to simply reflect the character of Christ on earth by way of living a life that upholds his glory and his teachings. The goal is to have absolute authority and power over every facet of human society." Brad Onishi (Terry Gross Interview). Christian Nationalism is the American form of Nazism. Read the full transcript of the Rise of Christian Nationalism at the QRCode in Table 3.2.

This is no longer a fringe movement. Many Republicans in Congress and the Courts have embraced this dangerous view (The most vocal are Mike Johnson, the Speaker of the House, Marjorie Taylor Green, Lauren Boebert, and Senator Josh Hawley). Donald Trump has embraced the promise to transform America from a representative democracy to a Christian Nationalist dictatorship.

The Christian Nationalist agenda is spelled out in the Republican "Project 2025" plan if Trump wins. At the heart of the plan is the conversion of the America Polity to a Christian Nationalist dictatorship. Make no mistake about it, Christian Nationalism is the enemy of the American people and only the Pro-Democracy Coalition can stop it.

WARNING! Kevin Roberts from the Heritage Foundation, a MAGA extremist, is threatening all who disagree with him with violence. He is no longer an American but an advocate of dictatorship.

The president of the Heritage Foundation on Tuesday declared that a new revolution is already underway in the U.S., appearing to warn Liberals that violence could erupt if they tried to stop it.

Kevin Roberts, whose uber-conservative think tank is behind the highly controversial "Project 2025" blueprint for a second Donald Trump presidency, made the comment during an appearance on Real America's Voice. "We are in the process of the second American Revolution, which will remain bloodless if the left allows it to be," Roberts said.

Heritage's Project 2025 calls for a huge increase in presidential power as well as a transformation of the federal government, replacing existing staffers with an army of those loyal to Trump. Roberts has previously said he sees his organization's role as ***"institutionalizing Trumpism."*** See Table 3.3 for the article by Dan Ladden-Hall.

Christian Nationalism's goals are written and spoken in plain sight of the American People. We must act in 2024 to stop these self-righteous, godless men who pervert Jesus's message of love because it is too "woke." And who are clearly un-American because they advocate dictatorship. These are self-appointed morality police who are agents of the worst kind of evil in the world. They are making a list of potential enemies of a Trumpian dictatorship. The chilling details of the Christian Nationalist agenda are outlined on sites provided in Table 3.3.

Table 3.3: QRCodes

Project 2025 Explained   2025 Threats of Violence

What is alarming is that at least 80 organizations, many new ones and a few older, traditional ones taken over by MAGA authoritarians, support Project 2025. They have pledged to accept an American dictatorship!

1. Alabama Policy Institute.
2. Alliance Defending Freedom.
3. America First Legal.
4. American Accountability Foundation.
5. American Association of Pro-Life Obstetricians and Gynecologists.
6. American Center for Law Justice.
7. American Compass.
8. American Cornerstone Institute.
9. American Council of Trustees and Alumni.
10. American Family Association.
11. American Family Project.
12. American Legislative Exchange Council (ALEC).
13. American Juris Link.
14. Association of Mature American Citizens.
15. American Moment.
16. American Principles Project.
17. California Family Council.
18. Center for Equal Opportunity.
19. Center for Family and Human Rights.
20. Center for Immigration Studies.
21. Center for Renewing America.
22. Claremont Institute.
23. Coalition for a Prosperous America.
24. Competitive Enterprise Institute.
25. Concerned Women for America.
26. Conservative Partnership Institute.
27. Defense of Freedom Institute.
28. Ethics and Public Policy Center.
29. Family Policy Alliance.
30. Family Research Council.
31. Feds for Medical Freedom.

32. First Liberty Institute.
33. Forge Leadership Network.
34. Foundation for American Innovation.
35. Foundation for Defense of Democracies.
36. Foundation for Government Accountability.
37. Frederick Douglass Foundation.
38. FreedomWorks.
39. Heartland Institute.
40. Heritage Foundation.
41. Hillsdale College.
42. Honest Elections Project.
43. Independent Women's Forum.
44. Institute for Education Reform.
45. Institute for Energy Research.
46. Institute for the American Worker.
47. Institute for Women's Health.
48. Intercollegiate Studies Institute.
49. James Madison Institute.
50. Job Creators Network.
51. Keystone Policy.
52. Liberty University.
53. Media Research Center.
54. Mississippi Center for Public Policy.
55. Moms for Liberty.
56. National Association of Scholars.
57. National Center for Public Policy Research.
58. Noah Webster Educational Foundation.
59. Oklahoma Council of Public Affairs.
60. Pacific Research Institute.
61. Patrick Henry College.
62. Personnel Policy Operations.
63. Project 21 Black Leadership Network.
64. Public Interest Legal Foundation.
65. Recovery for America Now Foundation.
66. Susan B. Anthony Pro-Life America.
67. Tea Party Patriots.
68. Teneo Network.

69. Texas Public Policy Foundation.
70. The Federalist Society.
71. The Foundation for Liberty and American Greatness (FLAG).
72. Thomas More Society.
73. Turning Point USA.
74. United States Justice Foundation.
75. Urban Reform Institute.
76. U.S. Justice Foundation.
77. Washington Policy Center.
78. Wisconsin Institute for Law & Liberty.
79. Young America's Foundation.
80. Youth for Western Civilization.

Fascist Right. Donald Trump has from the beginning of his candidacy been the champion for the Alt Right, and they have embraced him wholeheartedly. Groups like the Boogaloo Bois, the Proud Boys, the Three Percenters, and the Wolverine Watchmen who in the past have advocated a violet overthrow of the US Government are now preparing to be Trump's Militia if he wins and to react violently if he loses. They are now an integral part of the MAGA coalition.

The Morbidly Rich. Greed makes strange associations and many in the Billionaire Class are joining forces with the Christian Nationalists and the Authoritarian Right to help Trump. American policies, especially Democratic policies, do not reflect the relationship between the concentration of wealth and the rise of authoritarianism, a fact known in Ancient Greece. As more wealth is concentrated in the hands of fewer people, the appeal to authoritarianism from those who do not have much AND the billionaire class increases.

Robert Reich writes in his Substack (https://tinyurl.com/robertreich4) that "Elon Musk and entrepreneur and investor David Sacks reportedly held a secret billionaire dinner party in Hollywood last month [April 2024]. Its purpose: to defeat Joe Biden and reinstall Donald Trump in the White House. The guest list included Peter Thiel, Rupert Murdoch, Michael Milken, Travis Kalanick, and Steven Mnuchin, Trump's Treasury secretary."

These men will betray their country for a few dollars more. To put the magnitude of their wealth in perspective, each of these men has over

1,000 million dollars. The average size of the American High School is a little over 500 students. Imagine picking out two high schools and giving each student a million dollars.

Do the Morbidly Rich need more to be happy?

The Grifters. The final group actively supporting Trump and the Republicans are the grifters, minor and brazen alike. Trump, himself a world-class grifter, has opened the door to public coffers, to fraudulent campaign schemes, to influence peddling for profit, and to cheap and sleazy product sales over social media. (Gold tennis shoes, Non-Fungible Tokens (NFTs), wine, trading cards, coins, wine, steaks, chocolate and, of course, Trump University.)

The slate of Republicans running for public office these days has more than a few political and financial grifters on it. The model for this type of candidate is George Santos who was expelled from congress for falsely deceiving the electorate through massive lying, so he could receive the pension benefits of congressmen. This drain on our economy and political life must be reversed so that upright character, once again, is the ideal we strive for in our elected officials.

The Importance of Voting. For these reasons, the 2024 election is pivotal for America, a vote for Republicans is a vote for Christian Nationalism, more money for the Billionaire Class, mainstreaming the authoritarian right militia, ransacking public coffers and establishing an American dictatorship. The only way to preserve our democracy is to vote Democratic in all elections.

Only by having a Democratic President, a Democratic House and Senate can the scourge of Christian Nationalism and the greed of billionaires and grifters be checked. If they lose, Republicans have already said they will claim fraud, thus Democrats need to win big, so Republican false claims will be soundly rejected. In other words, the victory must be so large that the claim it was rigged will appear ridiculous.

If a candidate (Democrat, Republican, or Other) shows any of the behaviors of a dictator or embraces Christian Nationalism by word or deed, or stands to gain obscene windfall profits: Do NOT vote for him or her.

Why Democrats Now

Democrats are the anti-authoritarian party—the major party still embracing the Rule of Law and democratic governance. In this cycle, Democrats are leading the Pro-Democracy Coalition. The Republican Party has taken a dangerous tilt to authoritarianism and seeks to install a would-be dictator that serves only the interests of the powerful and Christinism cultists. The Republican Party is now beyond repair and must be voted into the trash-compacter of history.

What Democrats Stand For

Democratic Values (based on a Meta posting by Lori Gallagher Witt).

1. A country should take care of its weakest members. A country cannot call itself civilized when its children, disabled, sick, and elderly are neglected.
2. Healthcare is a right, not a privilege. Citizens cannot be free without their health.
3. The best investment a country can make is in education, which should be affordable and accessible to everyone.
4. The wealthy, who benefit from a stable and infrastructure-rich country, should pay their fair share of taxes.
5. Companies should pay their employees a liveable wage.
6. Given that many early colonists had fled to escape religious persecution and found haven in America, the long-standing freedom to practice one's religion and not a state-sponsored one is a bedrock principle. (The prohibition of a state religion is the first sentence in the first amendment to the US Constitution.)
7. All groups, no matter how different in their lifestyles, as long as they do not break the law, and they abide by the rule of law, have the same rights as any citizen of the country.
8. This country was founded by immigrants and since we are all immigrants or descended from immigrants, we value the contributions new immigrants make to the country.
9. The country is best served by a fair and open market economy with a level playing field, which requires regulation to prohibit monopolies and unfair business practices.
10. This country was founded on the rule of law and any form of authoritarianism is unacceptable and contrary to the Constitution.
11. The country has had a long and unjust history with other races, and if we are to live up to our motto on the Great Seal, "From

Many, One," we must continue to confront and to eliminate any vestiges of unjust treatment based on race.

12. The right to bear arms is in the Constitution, but the Constitution does not prohibit the regulation of arms, especially weapons of war, and therefore should be regulated to ensure the safety of our communities.

13. To function effectively, the country requires a level of decency among its citizens and a fundamental respect for one another.

14. Women and men are politically equal, and as men have final authority on their bodies, so do women.

15. We acknowledge the impact of humankind has had on the environment and as the chief custodian of the planet, humans have an obligation to address climate change for current and future generations.

Democratic Issues

A Sample of Democratic Issues (Based on the Progressive Change Institute Poll of 2016 Likely Voters.) All of these issues are supported by more Americans than those who oppose them.

- Allow Government to Negotiate Drug Prices.
- Ban For-Profit Prisons.
- Ban Revolving Door For Corporate Execs In Government.
- Break Up the Big Banks.
- Close Carried-Interest Tax Loophole.
- Close Offshore Corporate Tax Loopholes.
- Comprehensive Voter Empowerment Act.
- Debt-Free College At All Public Universities.
- Disclose Corporate Spending on Politics/Lobbying.
- End Gerrymandering.
- End Tax Deductions For Wall Street Fines.
- End Tax Loopholes for Corporations That Ship Jobs Overseas.
- Fair Trade That Protects Workers, the Environment, and Jobs.
- Free Community College.
- Free, High-Quality Public Child Care.
- Full Employment Act.
- Full Minimum Wage For Tipped Workers.
- Give Students The Same Low-Interest Rates As Big Banks.
- Green New Deal – Millions Of Clean-Energy Jobs.
- Increase the Minimum wage to a livable wage.

- Infrastructure Jobs Program.
- Let Homeowners Pay Down Mortgage With 401k.
- Medicare Buy-In For All.
- Protect and Expand Social Security Benefits.
- Public Funding Of Congressional Elections.
- Public Option Banking Via Post Offices.
- Require the separation of commercial and investment banking.
- Require NSA To Get Warrants.
- Require Special Prosecutor For Killings By Police.
- Restrict Surplus Military Equipment to Police Departments.
- Retrain Coal Miners And Oil Workers For Clean Energy Jobs.
- Shareholder Approval For Corporate Political Spending.
- Single Payer Healthcare Via Medicare.
- Tax the Rich at the 50% Reagan Rate.
- Transparency in Trade Negotiations.
- Universal Pre-Kindergarten.

Republican Issues

One key policy issue divides Republicans (Old and MAGA alike) and Democrats: taxation. Democrats believe that everyone should carry a fair share of societal costs. Without roads, without stability and security, without consumer protection, without a healthy citizenry, without a stable and fair banking system—no business can survive, let alone thrive.

Consider countries with no functioning governments, like Haiti and Somalia. The costs of starting and running a business are prohibitive. Sound government and responsible taxation with proceeds invested in public infrastructure and the public's good reduce the costs of business.

The Republicans want to lower taxes but every proposal they put forward gives those in the highest income brackets, those who need money the least, the most benefits. They also want to restrict going after wealthy tax cheats by eliminating funding to the IRS for tax auditors.

Bias to the wealthy is built into the Republican Party because many of its leaders are beholden to the wealthy and agree with many of them that the sole aim in life is to make money, even at the expense of the public good. Just-minded individuals are repelled at the obscene accumulation of wealth. How much money is enough for one person in a democracy?

A Sample of MAGA Republican Issues (Based on Story by SerenaTactics in Trends & Tactics)

- Ban Comprehensive Sex Education.
- Ban Critical Race Theory in Schools.
- Ban Voting Rights Expansions.
- Ban Sanctuary Cities.
- Ban Gun Control Measures.
- Ban the Green New Deal and Climate Regulations.
- Ban Abortion Rights.
- Ban Union Powers.
- Ban Government-Mandated Vaccinations.
- Ban Harm Reduction Sites for Drug Users.
- Ban Social Media Content Regulations.
- Ban Federal Funding for Sanctuary Universities.
- Ban Expansion of Mail-In Voting.
- Ban The Teaching of Evolution and Climate Change.
- Ban Plastic Bag Restrictions.
- Ban Public Broadcasting Funding.
- Ban Statehood for D.C. and Puerto Rico.
- Ban Net Neutrality Regulations.
- Ban Federal Minimum Wage Increases.
- Ban The Affordable Care Act (Obamacare).
- Ban National Monuments and Public Lands.
- Ban on Offshore Drilling Restrictions.
- Ban Consumer Privacy Laws.
- Ban High-Capacity Magazine Restrictions.
- Ban Affirmative Action Policies.
- Ban Federal Arts Funding.
- Ban Voice of America.

Republican Utah Senator Mike Lee's consistent view of safety net programs is captured during his 2010 campaign for senate. "I'm here right now to tell you one thing you probably have never heard from a politician: It will be my objective to phase out Social Security, to pull it up from the roots and get rid of it," Lee said during a campaign stop February 23, 2010, in Cache Valley, Utah.

"People who advise me politically always tell me it's dangerous and I tell them, 'In that case it's not worth my running.' That's why I'm doing this, to get rid of that. Medicare and Medicaid are of the same sort, they need to be pulled up." The video was originally recorded by YouTube user Michelle King in 2010, who Lee addressed by name during that same campaign event. (Nick Mordowanec, story for Newsweek Nov 3, 2022.)

Republican Senator Rick Scott proposes a 11 Point Plan to implement if Republicans gain control of Congress and the White House. "All federal legislation [including Social Security and Medicare] sunsets in 5 years. If a law is worth keeping, Congress can pass it again."

"Sen. Ron Johnson (R-Wis.) has suggested that Social Security and Medicare be eliminated as federal entitlement programs, and that they should instead become programs approved by Congress on an annual basis as discretionary spending." (Amy B Wang The Washington Post, Aug 3, 2022.)

############

No democracy can long survive which does not accept as fundamental to its very existence the recognition of the rights of minorities. FRANKLIN ROOSEVELT

We are of course a nation of differences. Those differences don't make us weak. They're the source of our strength. JIMMY CARTER

America is not like a blanket—one piece of unbroken cloth, the same color, the same texture, the same size. America is more like a quilt—many patches, many pieces, many colors, many sizes, all woven and held together by a common thread. JESSE JACKSON

* * *

THE ART OF VOTING

Voting as the Currency of Citizenship

Voting is the backbone of a democracy. Although it is necessary for a democracy, it is not sufficient for one. The voting process must be fair, inclusive and trustworthy. The act of voting is so important for legitimacy, that most dictatorships continue the process even though it has no meaning. Dictators completely control the process so they never lose.

One common route to dictatorship is for uninformed citizens to vote for a candidate whose intentions are to undermine a country's constitution and to consolidate power into his or her hands. Dictators count on low-information voters. So, in a true democracy, all citizens need to take the responsibility to vote seriously and become high-information voters or risk losing their democracy.

Even if we believe that our vote does not count or that we do not have enough time to vote, we should look at voting and the research required to make informed votes as the currency of citizenship. By voting, we preserve the freedom we enjoy and the form of government that has provided it to us. This is the best investment we can make and a small price to pay for our freedom.

Qualifications to Vote

The Constitution determines who is a citizen of the United States and only citizens may vote. Everyone must follow a two-step process before voting. Step 1: Determine if the applicant may vote at his or her residency (State, County, Municipality). This requires that the applicant register as a member of one of the authorized parties in the state (typically, Democrat, Republican, Libertarian, Green Party, or Unaffiliated). Step 2: On election day, the voter goes to the authorized polling station for the area (often called a precinct), presents an ID (in many states) and a poll worker will verify the voter's registration and current address of residency. Only then will the voter be given a ballot to cast a vote. (Early voting and absentee voting are variations on this process.)

The following list itemizes the qualifications to vote in the United States and applicants must meet all these qualifications before they can be registered.

1. *Be a citizen of the United States.* A person is a citizen if he or she was born within the United States, regardless of the citizenship status of their parents. If born outside the United States and at least one of the parents is a citizen, the child acquires citizenship. A resident can become a citizen through naturalization. The applicant must be 18 and have legal permanent resident status (green card) for at least five years or at least three years if applying as a spouse of a U.S. citizen.

   All naturalized citizens must take an oath of allegiance to the United States and pledge to support and defend the Constitution of the United States. Additionally, serving in the U.S. military can provide a means for expedited citizenship under the Immigration and Nationality Act (INA).

2. *Be 18 years old on or before Election Day to vote.* This requirement was set by the 26th Amendment.

3. *Be a resident of the state and county where voter intends to vote.* For North Carolina, residency for voting requires residing in the state and the voting precinct for at least 30 days before the election date. (Active Duty personnel stationed oversees have special rights.) Note: North Carolina has different residency requirements for other purposes, such as in-state tuition and driver's licenses.

4. *Not be serving a felony sentence, including any period of probation, post-release supervision, or parole.* Once their period of supervision is over, a person convicted of a felony automatically regains the right to vote. He or she must still register to vote, even if previously registered to vote prior to being convicted of a felony.

5. *College or university students.* Students may register and vote in the county where they go to school if they are physically present in the school community and do not intend to return to their former homes after graduation. However, if students intend to return to their former homes after graduation, they should remain registered in their hometowns.

More details about who can register to vote may be found by following the QRCode link in Table 4.1.

Table 4.1: QRCodes

Who Can Register

https://www.ncsbe.gov/
registering/who-can-register

Library of Congress Digital ID:
yan 1a38395 https://hdl.loc.gov/
loc.pnp/yan.1a38395

STEP 1: Registration

Registration can be viewed as the "pre-qualification" to vote, so poll workers do not need time to examine the voter's qualifications on election day. (However, a voter may register during the early voting period at the polls.) Registration is the "certification of eligibility" to vote.

The voter must be registered to vote in the state of his or her residence. On-line and mail registration must be completed (postmarked) 25 days before Election Day (5 November 2024), which is 11 October 2024 at 5:00.pm. After this deadline, registration is available only in-person during the early voting period, which for the November 2024 election, is 17 October 2024 to 2 November 2024. The deadline for military or overseas voters is 5 p.m. on the day before the election.

A voter has the choice of registering for any one of the five officially recognized parties in NC: Democrat, Green, Libertarian, Republican, and No Labels. The voter also has the option of registering as Unafiliated (UA). Registering for a political party gives the voter the right to vote in the party's primary when candidates are selected for the General Election.

NC has a semi-closed primary election system. This means unaffiliated voters may vote in a primary without having to change their affiliation but must pick one, and only one, party primary to vote in. In the General Election, Unaffiliated voters, like any registered voter may vote for any candidate on the ballot.

In NC, many local and municipal elections are nonpartisan, which means candidates do not run on official party tickets. (The notable exception is the County Board, which is selected through partisan elections.) There are no primary elections in non-partisan elections, so party designation is irrelevant.

To check registration status, voters should navigate to the website at the QRCode in Table 4.2 or check iwillvote.com.

Table 4.2: QRCodes

Am I Registered?

https://vt.ncsbe.gov/RegLKup/

Library of Congress Digital ID: ppmsca 19168 //hdl.loc.gov/ loc.pnp/ppmsca.19168

Several things to note about visiting the registration lookup site. Information is not case-sensitive. But the voter must use his or her formal name, for example "James," instead of "Jim." It may be necessary to try several iterations of the voter's name to make sure it is listed. Providing the least amount of information, first and last name only, improves the chances of finding the registration. Leave out middle initial, year of birth and county on the first try. The search will return a list of names that match the voter's name. This list can then be searched visually for one's registration by year of birth and county.

There are four ways a citizen can register to vote but each of these ways requires that he or she fill out a registration form that asks for the following information:

- Confirmation that the applicant is a U.S.citizen and meets the age requirements.
- Legal first name, last name, and suffix (if applicable).
- Date of birth.
- One of the following:
  1. An identification number: N.C. driver's license number, NCDMV ID number OR the last four digits of the applicant's Social Security Number.
  2. If the applicant does not have one of these forms of identification, he or she must check the box confirming that they do not have one.
- Residential address, including street number, name, and type, and unit number (if applicable), city, zip code, and county.
- Mailing address, if mail is not received at the residential address.
- Signature and date attesting to qualifications to vote.

Each of the four ways to register is relatively easy, but if the applicant needs help see page 36 for two telephone numbers to call for guidance. It is best to register as early as possible to have time to correct errors should they arise, and not wait until the early voting period to register when correction time is limited.

1. FIRST WAY: If the applicant has a NC driver's license, he or she can register Online at NC Division of Motor Vehicles (NCDMV). See Table 4.6

2. SECOND WAY: The applicant may register in person at any DMV site in the state or in person at any of the sites for the following state agencies:
   - Division of Services for the Blind
   - Division of Services for the Deaf and Hard of Hearing
   - Division of Health Benefits
   - Division of Child and Family Well-Being / WIC
   - Division of Social Services
   - Division of Rehabilitation Services
   - Division of Employment Security (DES)
   - Division of State Operated Healthcare Facilities

3. THIRD WAY: The applicant may register at the County Board of Elections either in person or by mail.

- Download and complete the appropriate voter registration application. Make sure to complete all required fields. (See Table 4.4)
- English N.C. Voter Registration Application (fillable PDF)
- Spanish N.C. Voter Registration Application (fillable PDF)
- Print the application.
- Sign the application (ink to paper). If the applicant is a *new registrant*, he or she must submit the original application by mail or in person. If the applicant is an *existing registrant* in the county and is using the form to update information, the signed form may be faxed or emailed.
- Mail the form to the county board of elections. (Mailing addresses are in the forms at QR Codes in Table 4.4).

NOTE 1: If the voter gives the signed application to another person or organization to submit on the voter's behalf, be sure the person or organization can commit to timely submitting the application to the proper board of elections.

Table 4.3: QRCodes

NC DMV Registration

https://www.ncdot.gov/dmv /offices-services/online/Pages/ voter-registration-application.aspx

Library of Congress Digital ID: yan 1a38536 https://hdl.loc.gov /loc.pnp/yan.1a38536

NOTE 2: During election season, voter registration volunteers set up tables or knock on neighborhood doors to identify and to assist those who are not yet registered. They can provide forms and assist in filling out the forms. They DO NOT advise on party affiliation and DO NOT retain any information from their assistance. Applicants are responsible for mailing or delivering their applications to the County Board of Elections.

Table 4.4: QRCodes

Registration Form (English)

https://s3.amazonaws.com
/dl.ncsbe.gov/Voter_Registration/
NCVoterRegForm_06W.pdf

Registration Form (Spanish)

https://s3.amazonaws.com/
dl.ncsbe.gov/Voter_Registration
/NCVoterRegForm_09W.pdf

4. FOURTH WAY: The applicant may register in person at his or her polling site during the early voting period. This is often referred to as same-day registration. **NOTE: Applicants may not register on election day.** Same-day registrants must attest to their eligibility and provide proof of where they live. A voter attests to his/her eligibility by completing and signing the North Carolina voter registration application as described in STEP 1: Registration above. Registering at an early voting site during the early voting period requires voters to provide proof of residence. Proof of residence includes any of the following documents with the voter's current address:

- North Carolina driver's license.
- Other photo identification issued by a government agency, provided that the card includes the voter's current name and address.
- A copy of a current utility bill, bank statement, government check, paycheck, or other government document showing the voter's name and address.
- For students living on campus, a document from an educational institution with the student's name and on-campus

housing address. Or, an educational institution may pro- vide the county board of elections a list of students residing in particular campus housing, which will suffice if a stu- dent living in campus housing shows a valid student photo identification card.

Within two business days of the person's registration, the county board of elections will verify the registrant's driver's license or Social Security number, update the voter registration database, search for possible duplicate registrations, and begin to verify the registrant's address by mail. The registrant's ballot will be counted unless the county board of elections determines that he or she is not qualified to vote in accordance with North Carolina law.

One of the voter suppression tactics adopted by the Republican Party is to challenge voter registration rolls in an attempt to disqualify vot- ers simply because their information is outdated or incorrect. **Voters should check their registration status well before the November election.**

Two useful numbers to help the applicant through the registration process:

- Vote@orangecountync.gov, or call 919-245-2350.
- Voter Assistance Hotline 1-833-868-3462.

Two sites provide information about how to register, the first is the NC State Board of Elections site, and the other is the Orange County Democratic Party site. Scan the QRCodes in Table 4.5 to navigate to these sites.

Registration is necessary, and it saves problems at the polling station if voter's data, especially the current address, are accurately reflected in the registration file.

During rregistration some applicants give little thought to party choice, opting instead for Unafilliated status. Not picking a party and register- ing as an unaffiliated voter is a convenient way to vote without joining a party. The voter may also vote in any primary to help a candidate from that party to advance to the general election.

Table 4.5: QRCodes

State Registration Help

https://www.ncsbe.gov/
registering/how-register

County Registration Help

https://www.orangedems.com/
resources/register/

However, there are disadvantages to registering as unaffiliated. To work in a party structure or to run as a party candidate except for municipal (and other non-partisan elections), a voter will need to register with that party.

Beyond these advantages, parties have a philosophy and a vision of how our society should be organized and run. Choosing and working within a party structure allows the voter to help elect those who will advance this vision. A citizen can only be a "player" in our society by picking a party and actively participating in it.

Registration status may be changed any time but will need to be made 25 days before an election when mailing or submitting it on-line to be recognized at the polls, otherwise party affiliation and other information may be changed during the early voting period at the polls.

STEP 2: Casting Votes

Election Eligibility Anyone who is a resident of North Carolina may vote in federal statewide races, such as those for the presidency and congressional senators, and for NC statewide elections, such as offices for Governor, Lt. Governor, Council of State, and Supreme Court.

However, for any offices defined by districts, like congressional house seats, NC General Assemble house and senate seats, county commissioners, mayors and town councils, school boards and other local offices, the precinct one lives in determines which of these district races the voter may vote in.

The County Board of Elections is responsible for printing the ballot "styled" for each precinct. This is one reason why having an accurate home address is so important for the voting process. This is also a good reason to get a sample ballot for the precinct, so the voter will know who will be on the ballot. This is especially important during presidential elections because so many "down ballot" offices may be overlooked.

Early Voting

Early voting (In-Person) or One-Stop Absentee Voting. Until recently most states have made it easier to vote. One such effort was to allow a period for early voting that typically ran two or more weeks before election day. But instead of voting at the regular precinct polling station for election day, votes are cast in specially designated early voting sites. (NOTE: This has caused confusion for some voters who vote early, for example in the primary, but vote on election day for the general election. It is likely that they will not be voting at the same site.) See Section Where to Vote for early voting sites in the county.

The in-person early voting period for the 2024 general election begins the third Thursday before election day, which is Thursday, Oct. 17, 2024 and ends the Saturday before Election day, which is 3 p.m., Nov. 2, 2024. Polls will be open weekdays from 8 am to 7:30 pm, Saturday from 8 am to 3 pm, and Sunday from 12 to 5 pm. Voters must show an acceptable photo ID (picture must resemble the voter and the name on the ID is the same or is very similar to the voter's name in their registration record). The address on the photo ID does not have to match the voter registration records. See page 49 for a list of acceptable IDs. If the voter has no acceptable ID, the voter may still proceed to vote in two ways:

1. Complete an ID Exception Form and then vote with a provisional ballot, or

2. Vote with a provisional ballot and then return to the county board of elections office with a photo ID by the day before the county canvass. (For municipal elections in September and October, this deadline is the Monday following Election Day. For all other

elections, the deadline is the second Thursday following Election Day.)

Election Day

Election-day voting (in-Person). Most votes are still cast on election day, which was established in 1845 as the first Tuesday after the first Monday in November. Each state sets open and closing times for the polls, which in North Carolina is from 6:30 AM to 7:30 PM, but voters in line at 7:30 PM will still be allowed to vote.

States are organized into voting precincts. Across the country there are approximately 168,000 precincts; as of 2024, North Carolina has around 2950 and Orange County has 40. All those residing in a precinct must vote at the designated voting site for that precinct. The voting sites for Orange County are listed in the Section Where to Vote.

As in early voting, voters must show an acceptable photo ID (picture must resemble the voter and the name on the ID is the same or is very similar to the voter's name in their registration record). The address on the photo ID does not have to match the voter registration records. See page 49 for a list of acceptable IDs. If the voter has no acceptable ID, the voter may still proceed to vote in two ways:

1. Complete an ID Exception Form and then vote with a provisional ballot, or

2. Vote with a provisional ballot and then return to the county board of elections office with a photo ID by the day before county canvass. (For municipal elections in September and October, this deadline is the Monday following Election Day. For all other elections, the deadline is the second Thursday following Election Day.)

Mail-In Voting

Mail-in or Absentee voting. States define their mail-in voting process. In North Carolina, voting by mail requires three steps: requesting, completing, and returning a ballot.

Requesting a Ballot. Registered voters must fill out a request form either on-line or on-paper from a downloaded form and send the completed

Table 4.6: QRCodes

NC DMV Registration

https://www.ncdot.gov/dmv
/offices-services/online/Pages/
voter-registration-application.aspx

Library of Congress Digital ID:
yan 1a38536 https://hdl.loc.gov
/loc.pnp/yan.1a38536

request to the voter's county Board of Elections. The county will verify the request and return a ballot (once they have been printed) to the address listed on the ballot request. The voter fills out the ballot and returns it in a timely fashion either by mailing or delivering it in person to the county Board of Elections.

NOTE: All voters must request a ballot either electronically or by paper, *but only military and overseas voters and voters with disabilities will receive AND submit their absentee ballots electronically.* Everyone else receives a paper ballot and either mails or delivers it to the county Board of Elections.

There are two ways to submit the ballot request form to the county Board of Elections: Online and On Paper.

ONLINE Absentee Portal

Option 1: *Request an Absentee Ballot electronically.* All registered North Carolina Voters may use this option to request an absentee-by-mail ballot. The online form that is filled out is sent to the voter's county board of elections office for processing. When the ballot is available for the election, it will be mailed to the address provided on the form. The deadline to request an absentee ballot is 5:00 PM the Tuesday before Election Day, which for 2024 is October 29. Visually impaired voters who would like to request an accessible ballot will also use Option 1 to submit their request

Option 2: *Access Military/Overseas Voter Services.* Active military, spouses or dependents of an active military service members or US citizens outside the United States, may use this option to request absentee ballots AND once approved, access ballots through this option. The deadline for a military/overseas voter to request an absentee ballot is 5:00 PM the day before Election Day.

Option 3: *Accessible Ballot.* Visually impaired voters who have requested an accessible (online) ballot and have been informed that their ballot is available, may select this option to access their ballot. If visually impaired voters would like to learn more about how this option works before accessing their ballots, they may navigate to the Ballot Portal at Table 4.7 and select Option 4 to practice with a demonstration ballot. The deadline to complete and return the absentee by mail ballot in the portal is 7:30 PM on Election Day.

Blind or visually impaired voters who need assistance with the absentee portal, may contact Allison Blackman, ADA Coordinator, at ADACoordinator@ncsbe.gov, (919) 814-0705, 6400 Mail Service Center, Raleigh, NC 27699-6400.

Option 4: *Sample Ballot.* Voters may use this option to view the contests and candidates specific to their eligible ballot. They may also mark and download a sample ballot. This allows voters to practice on their ballot forms before submitting their actual votes.

Table 4.7: QRCodes

NC Absentee Ballot Portal

Ballottrax

https://votebymail.
ncsbe.gov/app/home

https://northcarolina.
ballottrax.net/voter/

Completing the form online and submitting it to the NCSBE through the NC Absentee Ballot Portal completes the electronic request for an Absentee Ballot. Once the voter has requested an absentee ballot, its status can be tracked from printed to acceptance by signing up online for status notifications through BallotTrax. BallotTrax will be available 30 days prior to each election in 2024. See QRCode in Table 4.7 for BallotTrax.

ON PAPER

The voter can download a ballot request form, fill it out and submit it to the county Board of Elections. Navigate to the sites in Table 4.8 to download a PDF version (English or Spanish) to fill out.

Table 4.8: QRCodes

NC Ballot Request (English)   NC Ballot Request (Spanish)

https://s3.amazonaws.com/
dl.ncsbe.gov/Forms/2024/
English-Fillable-2024-Absentee
-Ballot-Request-Form.pdf

https://s3.amazonaws.com
/dl.ncsbe.gov/Forms/2024/
Spanish-Fillable-2024-Absentee
-Ballot-Request-Form.pdf

Completing the Ballot. County Boards of Elections start mailing absentee ballots on September 6, 2024. In NC, like many other states with Republican dominated legislatures, stringent requirements have been imposed on mail-in ballots.

Absentee voters are required to mark their ballots in the presence of two witnesses or one notary public. Anyone 18 or over may be a witness, including spouses and other family members. These witnesses must not observe choices made on the ballot.

The voter is also required to include a photocopy of a photo ID inside the return envelope that comes with the ballot. See page 49 for acceptaible forms of ID. If the voter does not have an acceptable form of ID, he/she may complete an ID Exception Form and submit it with the ballot.

Once the ballot is completed the following three steps are necessary.

1. Seal the ballot and ID envelope in the return envelope provided.

2. Complete and sign the Absentee Application and Certificate on the return envelope.

3. Have two witnesses (or one notary public) complete and sign the return envelope in the space designated as Witness's Certification.

This absentee voting summary is provided by NCvoter.org (https://ncvoter.ogr/absentee-ballots/).

Submitting the Ballot. After completing, submit the form in person to the county board of elections or by mail via the U.S. Postal Service, DHL, FedEx, or UPS. (See Ballot Request form for mailing addresses.) All absentee voters are required to submit a paper ballot unless they are military, an oversees voter, or disabled. These voters may cast their ballots electronically. See the Access Military/Overseas Voter Services section on page 41.

IMPORTANT: The mail-in ballot must be RECEIVED by the county Board of Elections by 7:30 pm, election day. A postmark date no longer counts.

North Carolina takes extensive measures to secure absentee balloting described at the URL in Table 4.9.

Provisional Voting

Provisional Voting on Election Day. A voter receives a provisional ballot when questions arise about:

- *No Record of Registration*: A voter's record of registration cannot be found in the voter registration list at the time the voter presents to vote at the voting site.
- *Unreported Move*: A voter provides an address different from the voter's registered address, and the voter indicates that the move to the new address occurred 30 or more days before Election Day.
- *Previously Removed*: A voter was previously registered in the

Table 4.9: QRCodes

Securing Absentee Voting

https://s3.amazonaws.com
/dl.ncsbe.gov/election
-security/facts/how-we-
secure-absentee-voting.pdf

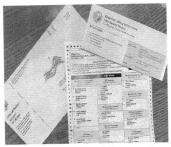

https://southerncoalition.org/
wp-content/uploads/2022/
04/1f924ae8-1951-499a-bdbf
-63eac198932b-IMG_3571
-scaled-1.jpeg

county but the registration was canceled. A voter's registration may be canceled for a number of reasons (moved within state; moved to another state; felony conviction; removed due to list maintenance; successful voter challenge; deceased, etc.).

- *No Acceptable ID*: A voter does not present acceptable identification under the Help America Vote Act (HAVA).
- *Unrecognized Address*: An election official is unable to locate a voter's address in the county's street lookup files.
- *Incorrect Precinct*: This provisional voting reason is used when a voter requests to vote at a polling place on Election Day that is not the vote's proper precinct. The voter's proper precinct is the precinct assigned to the voter based on residential address 30 or more days before Election Day.
- *Incorrect Party*: During a partisan primary, a voter insists on voting a ballot for a political party that the voter is not affiliated with.
- *Voter Already Voted*: A voter's record indicates that the voter has already cast a ballot in the election.
- *Jurisdiction Dispute*: A voter presents to vote and has no eligible ballot style or the voter requests to vote in a contest not in the voter's assigned voting district based on his or her legal voting residence.
- *Voted During Extended Hours*: The hours for voting are extended

by the State Board of Elections or a court order. Voters who cast a ballot during extended hours must vote a provisional ballot.

In 2020, 60% of provisional ballots cast were not counted. The greatest factors in provisional ballot rejection rates were registration (72%) and voting out of precinct (11%) (democracync.org).

A provisional ballot is also used when a voter does not or cannot present photo ID when voting in person. This is the reason voters should obtain a picture ID as soon as possible so they do not risk losing their vote.

Through provisional voting, all citizens have the opportunity to cast a ballot, even if questions arise. Provisional voting is fail-safe voting. State law mandates that no person shall be denied the option to vote a provisional ballot. In no circumstance should a voter be turned away.

If the problem is out-of-precinct voting (meaning the voter is in the right county, but the wrong precinct) the voter MUST BE GIVEN THE CHOICE to vote a provisional ballot at the polling place where they are OR go to their correct precinct where they will be able to vote a regular ballot (democracync.org).

If a voter who is out of precinct on Election Day was not given both choices (to go to their correct precinct OR cast a provisional ballot), please call 888-OUR-VOTE (democracync.org).

If a voter is not able to cast a regular ballot, the voter will go to the Help Station for help casting a provisional ballot. The voter will receive a Help Referral Form explaining the reason for the referral to the Help Station.

An election official at the Help Station will help the voter complete a Provisional Voting Application and provide a provisional ballot and envelope. Then, the voter will complete the ballot in private, seal the ballot in the envelope and return the envelope to the Help Station.

Each provisional voter will receive a Provisional Identification Number (PIN). The voter can use this, along with their date of birth, to check the status of their provisional ballot. (This status will not be available earlier than 10 days after the date of the election.)

The election official will also inform the voter, if applicable, of any additional steps the voter must take to ensure their ballot counts.

To check the status of a provisional vote, check the QRC site at Table 4.10.

Table 4.10: QRCodes

Provisional Voting Status

https://vt.ncsbe
.gov/RegProvPIN

Library of Congress Digital ID:
yan 1a37912 https://hdl.loc
.gov/loc.pnp/yan.1a37912

OR call (919) 814-0700 or (866) 522-4723 (toll-free).

All provisional envelopes are returned to the county board of elections. County board of elections staff research details of provisional applications and the voters' eligibility. They then provide results to the county board of elections for final determination.

This process is often called "curation of conditional ballots" and refers to the process of managing, verifying, and validating provisional or conditional ballots cast during an election. For example, if a voter does not appear on the registration list but claims to have registered, elections officials will research to see if there was a registration attempt.

Provisional voters can help "curate" or supply/correct the information leading to problems with their eligibility on election day instead of waiting for the Board of Election's determination. Here are some actions that can be taken to ensure the provisional ballot is approved.

- Follow the status of the provisional vote by going to the QRCode for the URL in Table 4.10.

- Contact the county Board of Elections by phone to provide additional information or determine what is missing.
- Visit the county Board of Elections and give them missing or corrected information.
- After providing additional information, follow up online to make sure the provisional ballot has been counted.

No election results are finalized until determination of the statuses of the provisional ballots has been made.

The decision to count in full, partially count, or not count a provisional ballot is made during the statewide Canvass, which takes place 10 days after Election Day. Each CBOE will meet on this day to vote on provisional ballots; any voter may attend the Canvass (democracync.org).

If a provisional application is approved, only then will the voter's provisional ballot be removed from the sealed envelope and the ballot counted or, if applicable, partially counted. Ballots are partially counted if a provisional voter was not entitled to vote for all contests on the ballot.

If a provisional application is not approved, the ballot remains sealed in the provisional envelope.

Additional Voter Information

Help for voters with disabilities. Federal and state laws require early voting locations and Election Day polling sites to be accessible. In addition to making polling places accessible to voters, the State Board of Elections strives to provide voters with options if they are unable to make it inside the polling place to vote.

Through curbside voting, a voter can cast a ballot while in a vehicle outside the polling location. Some sites also provide a walk-up area for curbside voting in addition to the drive-up area. Curbside voting is offered at all Election Day polling and early voting sites. Curbside voters must sign an affidavit affirming that they are unable to enter the voting place to cast their ballot. A curbside voter has the same rights to assistance as any other voter.

If the voter is blind or visually impaired, he/she may request, mark, and return an accessible absentee ballot online through the N.C. Absentee Ballot Portal (see Accessible Ballot on page 41). It is compatible with screen readers and accepts a digital or typed signature.

If the voter lives at a facility such as a hospital, clinic, or nursing home, assistance is available with mail-in voting and other services provided by a multi-partisan assistance team (MAT) at Assistance for Voters in Care Facilities. See Table 4.11 for URL.

Table 4.11: QRCodes

Assisted Living Voter Assistance

https://www.ncsbe.gov /voting/help-voters-disabilities/ assistance-voters-care-facilities

Image generated by ChatGPT 4.0
Image Generator by Naif Alotaibi

Voting Equipment. All voting systems in North Carolina use paper ballots, marked either by hand or with a ballot-marking device, providing a paper trail of votes cast at polling sites that can be audited or recounted by elections officials. Military and overseas voters, as well as visually impaired voters, can request, access, and submit an absentee ballot through a secure online portal (see Access Military/Overseas Voter Services on page 41).

All 100 counties comply with federal law by having ballot-marking devices available at every polling place for any voter who needs or wishes to use one to mark a ballot independently. All counties in North Carolina currently use either ES&S or Hart equipment. Under state law, voting equipment may not be connected to the internet or use wireless access, limiting the possibility of outside interference. More details about the voting equipment used in NC can be found at the NCSBE site shown in Table 4.12.

Table 4.12: QRCodes

Voting Equipment

https://www.ncsbe.gov/
voting/voting-equipment

Electronic Systems & Software DS200
Optical Scan Vote-Counting Machine

Picture Identification. As noted several times previously, voters must have a picture ID that they can present at polling stations. The following ID's are acceptable as long as they are valid and unexpired.

- North Carolina driver's license.
- State ID from the NCDMV (also called "non-operator ID").
- Driver's license or non-driver ID from another state, District of Columbia, or U.S. territory (only if voter registered in North Carolina within 90 days of the election).
- U.S. Passport or U.S. Passport card.
- North Carolina voter photo ID card issued by a county board of elections.
- College or university student ID approved by the State Board of Elections.
- State or local government or charter school employee ID approved by the State Board of Elections.
- A voter 65 or older may use an expired form of acceptable ID if the ID was unexpired on their 65th birthday.

Any of the following may be used, regardless of whether the ID contains an expiration or issuance date:

- Military or veterans ID card (with photo) issued by the U.S. government.
- Tribal enrollment card (with photo) issued by a tribe recognized

by the State of North Carolina or the federal government.
- ID card (with photo) issued by an agency of the U.S. government or the State of North Carolina for a public assistance program (Although this is an acceptable form of ID under North Carolina law, the State Board is not aware of any such ID in circulation that contains a photo. All IDs for voting are required to have a photo.)

Most people use a driver's license but if a voter does not have one, DMV, the State Board of Elections, or the County Board of Elections will provide a picture ID.

Voting for a Veteran. NC has a "Vote in Honor of a Veteran" Program that provides North Carolinians an opportunity to pay tribute to those who have served this country in the Armed Forces. Any voter can honor a veteran on any Election Day by requesting a pin. Pins are provided for free by the State Board of Elections. Each pin can be personalized with the name of the veteran a voter wishes to honor.

Table 4.13: QRCodes

Vote for a Veteran PIN

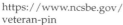

https://www.ncsbe.gov/
veteran-pin

Where to Vote

State law requires that voters vote in the county of their primary residence within the designated precinct, except for students who do not intend to return to their family residence. These voters can vote in the precinct encompassing their college residence. The Board of Elections for each county defines the boundaries for the precincts within the county and arranges a polling site within each precinct. The county also identifies a number of polling sites for early voting, which will typically be different from regular polling sites but on a rare occasion may be the same as an election day site for a precinct.

Both early voting sites and election day polling sites are listed on the county's website. For example, Orange County has 6 designated early voting sites for all 40 precincts. The 2024 early voting sites are the following:

1. Orange Works (BOE), 300 West Tryon Street, Hillsborough, NC 27278.
2. For 2024, 108 Bim Street, Carrboro, NC. After 2024, The new Southern Orange Library Bldg, 203 S. Greensboro ST. Carrboro, NC 27510.
3. Chapel of the Cross, 304 East Franklin Street, Chapel Hill, NC 27514.
4. Chapel Hill Library, 100 Library Drive, Chapel Hill, NC 27514
5. Eflands Cheeks Community Center, 117 Richmond Road, Efland, NC 27243.
6. Seymour Center, 2551 Homestead Road, Chapel Hill, NC 27516.

Voters from any precinct may vote in any early voting sites from 17 October to 2 November 2024, but MUST vote in their precinct polling station on election day.

Tables 4.14, 4.15, and 4.16 list the polling sites for each of the 40 precincts in Orange County.

Many counties maintain a GIS database matching voter addresses with precincts. Voters in Orange County who are unsure of their precinct may check the site at Table 4.17, which points to a map of the area. The voter need only select Voting Information and enter a street address in the input field to find their precinct.

Those using absentee ballots may take them to their County Board of Elections in person. For Orange County that address is: 208 S. Cameron Street, Hillsborough, NC 27278 OR mail them to: Orange County Board of Elections, P.O. Box 220, Hillsborough, NC 27278.

Table 4.14: Orange County Precincts

Precinct Name (Precinct Code)	Polling Site & Location	NC House District	Commissioner District
1 Caldwell (CW)	Caldwell Community Bldg 7607 NC 157N Rougemont	50	2
2 Carr (CA)	Cedar Grove Fire Station Number 1 5912 Pentecost Road Mebane	50	2
3 Carrboro (CB)	Carrboro Elem School 400 Shelton Street Carrboro	56	1
4 Cedar Falls (CF)	East Chapel Hill High School 500 Weaver Dairy Rd Chapel Hill	56	1
5 Cedar Grove (CG)	Cedar Grove Center 5800 NC HWY 86 N Hillsborough	50	2
6 Cheeks (CX)	Gravelly Hill Middle School 4801 W Ten Road Efland	50	2
7 Coker Hills (CH)	Church of Reconciliation 110 N Elliott Road Chapel Hill	56	1
8 Coles Store (CS1)	Union Grove Methodist Ch 6401 Union Grove Church Rd Hillsborough	50	2
9 Colonial Heights (CO)	Smith Middle School, 9201 Seawell School Road Chapel Hill	56	1
10 Damascus (DM)	Carrboro High School 201 Rock Haven Road Carrboro	56	1
11 Dogwood Acres (DA)	Mary Scroggs Elementary 501 Kildaire Road Chapel Hill	56	1
12 East Franklin (EA)	Holy Trinity Lutheran Ch 300 E Rosemary Street	56	1
13 Eastside (ES)	Ephesus Elementary 1495 Ephesus Church Rd Chapel Hill	56	1
14 Efland (EF)	Efland Ruritan Club 3009 Forrest Avenue Efland, NC 27243	50	2
15 Eno (E)	Palmers Grove UMC Bldg 1211 Palmers Grove Ch Rd Hillsborough	50	2
16 Estes Hills (EH)	Chapel Hill Public Lib Rm B 100 Library Drive Chapel Hill	56	1

Table 4.15: Orange County Precincts

Precinct Name (Precinct Code)	Polling Site & Location	NC House District	Commissioner District
17 Glenwood (GL)	Rashkis Elementary 601 Meadowmont Ln Chapel Hill	56	1
18 Grady Brown (GB)	Grady Brown Elem School 1100 New Grady B Sch Rd Hillsborough	50	2
19 Hillsborough (H)	Orange County Rec Center 302 W Tryon Street Hillsborough	50	2
20 Hillsborough East (HE)	Passmore Senior Center 103 Meadowlands Drive Hillsborough, NC	50	2
21 Hillsborough North (HN)	Orange Middle School Auditorium 308 Orange High School Rd. Hillsborough	50	2
22 Hogan Farms (HF)	Morris Grove Elem School 215 Eubanks Rd Chapel Hill	56	1
23 Kings Mill (KM)	UNC Finley Golf Clubhouse 500 Finley Golf Course Rd Chapel Hill, NC 27514	56	1
24 North Carrboro (NC)	Chapel Hill High School 1709 High School Road Chapel Hill,	56	1
25 Northside (NS)	First Baptist Church, 106 N Roberson Street Chapel Hill	56	1
26 Orange Grove (OG)	Cane Creek Church Center 6716 Orange Grove Rd Hillsborough	50	2
27 OWASA (OW)	OWASA Admin Bldg 400 Jones Ferry Road Carrboro	56	1
28 Patterson (PA)	New Hope Community Center 4014 Whitfield Road Chapel Hill	50	2
29 Ridgefield (RF)	Binkley Baptist Church 1712 Willow Drive Chapel Hill	56	1
30 Rogers Eubanks (RE)	Animal Services Meeting Rm 1601 Eubanks Rd Chapel Hill	56	1,2
31 St. John (SJ)	McDougle Middle School 900 Old Fayetteville Road Chapel Hill	56	1
32 St. Marys (SM)	New Sharon Methodist Ch 1601 New Sharon Ch Rd Hillsborough	50	2

Table 4.16: Orange County Precincts

Precinct Name (Precinct Code)	Polling Site & Location	NC House District	Commissioner District
33 Tolars (TO)	Schley Grange Hall 3416 Schley Road Hillsborough	50	2
34 Town Hall (TH)	Carrboro Town Hall 108 Bim Street Carrboro	56	1
35 UNC (U)	UNC Stone Center 150 South Road Chapel Hill	56	1
36 Weaver Dairy (WD)	Seymour Senior Center 2551 Homestead Rd Chapel Hill	50	1
37 Weaver Dairy Sat (WDS)	Carol Woods Retirement 750 Weaver Dairy Road Chapel Hill	50	1
38 West Hillsborough (WH)	Central Elementary Sch 154 Hayes Street Hillsborough	50	2
39 Westwood (WW)	Frank Porter Graham Sch 101 Smith Level Road Chapel Hill	56	1
40 White Cross (WC)	White Cross Fire Station 5722 Old Greensboro Rd Chapel Hill	50	2

Table 4.17: QRCodes

My Precinct Voting Site

https://aries.orangecounty
nc.gov/Aries/

When to Vote

As a democracy, we vote often. We vote for federal offices established by the US Constitution, for state offices established by state constitutions, and for local offices established by state legislatures. And we vote in almost every organization to which we belong.

Voting is a duty of each citizen to maintain our democracy but over the last 50 years a low of 52% to, most recently, a high of 67% of registered voters went to the polls. More participation is needed, but it should be done thoughtfully and respectfully to safeguard the constitution. Here is a general overview of the types of elections American citizens may expect.

Federal Elections Presidential elections are held every four years. Voters elect the President and the Vice-President of the United States through the Electoral College. The most recent presidential election was in 2020, so the next one is in 2024.

House members of Congress are elected for two-year terms, with elections held every even-number year. There are no staggered terms in the House, so all 435 seats in the House are up for election every two years.

Senators serve six-year terms and elections are staggered so that approximately one-third of the Senate is up for election every two years. This means Senate elections also occur during every federal election cycle, including both midterm and presidential election years.

State and Local Elections Most governors are elected every four years, though the timing and whether they coincide with presidential elections can vary by state. Some states hold gubernatorial elections during presidential years, while others have them during midterm years.

Most state legislators are elected every two years, though in some states, senators (the upper chambers) have four-year terms, and these can be staggered.

Mayoral, city council, county commissioners and other local government positions typically have varying terms and election cycles, which can range from two to four years, depending on the locality and specific office.

Midterm Elections Midterm elections are the elections held two years after the presidential vote. These elections generally do not attract a turnout as heavy as a presidential election. These elections include:

- All 435 seats in the U.S. House of Representatives.
- One-third of the U.S. Senate.
- Many state and local positions, including some gubernatorial elections.

Off-Year Elections These are elections that do not occur in the same years as federal congressional elections (that is, they are non-midterm, non-presidential). They often include local elections, such as those for mayors, city council members, and local judges. Some states like Virginia and New Jersey hold their gubernatorial and state legislative elections during off-years.

Special Elections Special elections are held at various times as needed to fill vacancies caused by deaths, resignations, or other unforeseen circumstances in any of the above institutions, ranging from the U.S. Congress to local city councils.

Selecting Candidates

There are many elections and many candidates to chose from. The starting point for a systematic review of candidates is to learn who is running in primary elections for the voter's party. Most of a voter's research will be focused on the primary elections to select candidates for the general election. Once the primary is over, party members will typically vote along party lines regardless of who won the primary. If the voter is unaffiliated, he or she will need to research all the party candidates to make an informed choice. Each county will provide sample ballots for both primary races and the general election.

Researching candidates should be thoughtful, but some people feel their effort will take too much time, and they use this as a reason not to vote. But there are ways to make it easier to pick candidates that align with one's position on key issues.

The biggest time saver for the general election is for voters to pick a party that aligns with their philosophy of governance and join it. The choices are reduced dramatically because the party, through its caucus or primary process, picks candidates that voters have selected to represent the point of view the party stands for (a party's position is formally stated in its "platform").

Another way to reduce the time to research individual candidates is to review literature and websites produced by civic organizations that encourage candidates to post information about themselves and their positions on many issues. The League of Women Votes provides a comprehensive site on candidate information (VOTE411.org).

Other organizations in the community provide similar platforms for candidates to express their views. For example, both the Raleigh News & Observer and the Charlotte Observer in N.C. produce Voter Guides. The State Board of Elections provides information on candidates running in the primary elections for NC Supreme Court and NC Court of Appeals.

Table 4.18: QRCodes

LWV Voter Guide

Orange County Sample Ballots

https://www.vote411
.org/ballot

https://www.orangecountync.
gov/1216/Sample-Ballots
-Maps-Voting-Location-Info

How to Vote and What You can Expect at the Polls

One of the most rewarding events in a democratic state is the act of voting. Most voters are moved in profound ways by casting a vote. It is a physical reminder that we live in a democracy and that we chose our leaders.

The most affected are often the newest American citizens who have never voted before in a real election because they have fled a dictatorship to join the American community. For many it is not only a duty, but a privilege, to vote.

If you are voting early, you will vote at one the designated early voting sites which probably will not be your precinct voting site for same-day voting. Make sure you have downloaded a sample ballot from the county site and have researched, and selected, the candidates you intend to vote for.

Make sure you bring an approved ID and if you intend to register as well as vote (only during early voting), bring a utility bill or other evidence of your residence within the precinct.

Once you arrive at the site you will likely be approached by representatives of the candidates or representatives of the political parties asking if you need more information to make up your mind. These conversations can be helpful if you have not yet decided on your choices. If you do not want to talk to them, wave off their advances or let them know that you have decided.

All candidates and political party workers must stay 25 ft from the polling station and cannot intimidate voters.

You will then join a line (during busy times) into the polling station. Once in the polling station you will be directed to a table where several poll workers will be checking registrations and issuing ballots. The poll worker will ask your name and confirm that you are registered, then ask you to confirm your address. If you are at the wrong precinct, you may be directed to the correct one or be given the option to vote a provisional ballot. You will be asked for your picture ID.

If there is an issue that needs resolving before you can vote, you may be offered a provisional ballot (see Provisional Voting on Election Day on page 45). Once cleared to vote, you will be asked to sign a form verifying your information. Then you will be given a paper ballot and a pencil with all the races that you are eligible to vote in, and directed to a voting station.

Once in the voting station, you cannot use your mobile phone, but you can refer to your sample paper ballot with your choices. Read the instructions carefully. Some races may require that you select multiple candidates. If you select multiple candidates where only one is required, your choices will be ignored in the final count. Fill out the real ballot by marking the bubbles next to your candidates of choice. Make sure that your mark is clear and completely fills the choice bubble.

After you have finished voting, take your ballot to the ballot box and insert it into the input feeder. Return your pencil and get your "I Voted" sticker.

Table 4.19: QRCodes

Voting Tools

https://www.ncsbe.gov/
voting/voter-tools-and-forms

Summary of Tools

The NC State Board of Election provides seven tools and 4 forms for voting. Many of these have been referenced elsewhere in this document, but the site at Table 4.19 lists them in one place.

* * *

APPENDIX I: The United States Constitution

We the People of the United States, in Order to form a more perfect Union, establish Justice, insure domestic Tranquility, provide for the common defense, promote the general Welfare, and secure the Blessings of Liberty to ourselves and our Posterity, do ordain and establish this Constitution for the United States of America.

Article I

Section 1: Congress.

All legislative Powers herein granted shall be vested in a Congress of the United States, which shall consist of a Senate and House of Representatives.

Section 2: The House of Representatives.

The House of Representatives shall be composed of Members chosen every second Year by the People of the several States, and the Electors in each State shall have the Qualifications requisite for Electors of the most numerous Branch of the State Legislature.

No Person shall be a Representative who shall not have attained to the Age of twenty-five Years, and been seven Years a Citizen of the United States, and who shall not, when elected, be an Inhabitant of that State in which he shall be chosen.

Representatives and direct Taxes shall be apportioned among the several States which may be included within this Union, according to their respective Numbers, which shall be determined by adding to the whole Number of free Persons, including those bound to Service for a Term of Years, and excluding Indians not taxed, three fifths of all other Persons. The actual Enumeration shall be made within three Years after the first Meeting of the Congress of the United States, and within every subsequent Term of ten Years, in such Manner as they shall by Law direct. The number of Representatives shall not exceed one for every thirty Thousand, but each State shall have at Least one Representative;

and until such enumeration shall be made, the State of New Hampshire shall be entitled to choose three, Massachusetts eight, Rhode-Island and Providence Plantations one, Connecticut five, New-York six, New Jersey four, Pennsylvania eight, Delaware one, Maryland six, Virginia ten, North Carolina five, South Carolina five, and Georgia three.

When vacancies happen in the Representation from any State, the Executive Authority thereof shall issue Writs of Election to fill such Vacancies.

The House of Representatives shall choose their Speaker and other Officers; and shall have the sole Power of Impeachment.

Section 3: The Senate.

The Senate of the United States shall be composed of two Senators from each State, chosen by the Legislature thereof, for six Years; and each Senator shall have one Vote.

Immediately after they shall be assembled in Consequence of the first Election, they shall be divided as equally as may be into three Classes. The Seats of the Senators of the first Class shall be vacated at the Expiration of the second Year, of the second Class at the Expiration of the fourth Year, and of the third Class at the Expiration of the sixth Year, so that one third may be chosen every second Year; and if Vacancies happen by Resignation, or otherwise, during the Recess of the Legislature of any State, the Executive thereof may make temporary Appointments until the next Meeting of the Legislature, which shall then fill such Vacancies.

No Person shall be a Senator who shall not have attained to the Age of thirty Years, and been nine Years a Citizen of the United States, and who shall not, when elected, be an Inhabitant of that State for which he shall be chosen.

The Vice President of the United States shall be President of the Senate, but shall have no Vote, unless they be equally divided.

The Senate shall choose their other Officers, and also a President pro tempore, in the Absence of the Vice President, or when he shall exercise the Office of President of the United States.

The Senate shall have the sole Power to try all Impeachments. When sitting for that Purpose, they shall be on Oath or Affirmation. When the President of the United States is tried, the Chief Justice shall preside: And no Person shall be convicted without the Concurrence of two thirds of the Members present.

Judgment in Cases of Impeachment shall not extend further than to removal from Office, and disqualification to hold and enjoy any Office of honor, Trust or Profit under the United States: but the Party convicted shall nevertheless be liable and subject to Indictment, Trial, Judgment and Punishment, according to Law.

Section 4: Elections.

The Times, Places and Manner of holding Elections for Senators and Representatives, shall be prescribed in each State by the Legislature thereof; but the Congress may at any time by Law make or alter such Regulations, except as to the Places of choosing Senators.

The Congress shall assemble at least once in every Year, and such Meeting shall be on the first Monday in December, unless they shall by Law appoint a different Day.

Section 5: Powers and Duties of Congress.

Each House shall be the Judge of the Elections, Returns and Qualifications of its own Members, and a Majority of each shall constitute a Quorum to do Business; but a smaller Number may adjourn from day to day, and may be authorized to compel the Attendance of absent Members, in such Manner, and under such Penalties as each House may provide.

Each House may determine the Rules of its Proceedings, punish its Members for disorderly Behavior, and, with the Concurrence of two thirds, expel a Member.

Each House shall keep a Journal of its Proceedings, and from time to time publish the same, excepting such Parts as may in their Judgment require Secrecy; and the Yeas and Nays of the Members of either House on any question shall, at the Desire of one fifth of those Present, be entered on the Journal.

Neither House, during the Session of Congress, shall, without the Consent of the other, adjourn for more than three days, nor to any other Place than that in which the two Houses shall be sitting.

Section 6: Rights and Disabilities of Members.

The Senators and Representatives shall receive a Compensation for their Services, to be ascertained by Law, and paid out of the Treasury of the United States. They shall in all Cases, except Treason, Felony and Breach of the Peace, be privileged from Arrest during their Attendance at the Session of their respective Houses, and in going to and returning from the same; and for any Speech or Debate in either House, they shall not be questioned in any other Place.

No Senator or Representative shall, during the Time for which he was elected, be appointed to any civil Office under the Authority of the United States, which shall have been created, or the Emoluments whereof shall have been increased during such time; and no Person holding any Office under the United States, shall be a Member of either House during his Continuance in Office.

Section 7: Legislative Process.

All Bills for raising Revenue shall originate in the House of Representatives; but the Senate may propose or concur with Amendments as on other Bills.

Every Bill which shall have passed the House of Representatives and the Senate, shall, before it become a Law, be presented to the President of the United States; If he approves he shall sign it, but if not, he shall return it, with his Objections to that House in which it shall have originated, who shall enter the Objections at large on their Journal, and proceed to reconsider it. If after such Reconsideration two thirds of that House shall agree to pass the Bill, it shall be sent, together with the Objections, to the other House, by which it shall likewise be reconsidered, and if approved by two thirds of that House, it shall become a Law. But in all such Cases the Votes of both Houses shall be determined by Yeas and Nays, and the Names of the Persons voting for and against the Bill shall be entered on the Journal of each House respectively. If any Bill shall not be returned by the President within ten Days (Sundays excepted) after it shall have been presented to him, the Same shall be a Law, in like Manner as if he had signed it, unless the Congress by their Adjournment prevent its Return, in which Case it shall not be a Law.

Every Order, Resolution, or Vote to which the Concurrence of the Senate and House of Representatives may be necessary (except on a question of Adjournment) shall be presented to the President of the United States; and before the Same shall take Effect, shall be approved by him, or being disapproved by him, shall be repassed by two thirds of the Senate and House of Representatives, according to the Rules and Limitations prescribed in the Case of a Bill.

Section 8: Powers of Congress.

The Congress shall have Power To lay and collect Taxes, Duties, Imposts and Excises, to pay the Debts and provide for the common defense and general Welfare of the United States; but all Duties, Imposts and Excises shall be uniform throughout the United States;

To borrow Money on the credit of the United States;

To regulate Commerce with foreign Nations, and among the several States, and with the Indian Tribes;

To establish a uniform Rule of Naturalization, and uniform Laws on the subject of Bankruptcies throughout the United States;

To coin Money, regulate the Value thereof, and of foreign Coin, and fix the Standard of Weights and Measures;

To provide for the Punishment of counterfeiting the Securities and current Coin of the United States;

To establish Post Offices and post Roads;

To promote the Progress of Science and useful Arts, by securing for limited Times to Authors and Inventors the exclusive Right to their respective Writings and Discoveries;

To constitute Tribunals inferior to the supreme Court;

To define and punish Piracies and Felonies committed on the high Seas, and Offenses against the Law of Nations;

To declare War, grant Letters of Marque and Reprisal, and make Rules concerning Captures on Land and Water;

To raise and support Armies, but no Appropriation of Money to that Use shall be for a longer Term than two Years;

To provide and maintain a Navy;

To make Rules for the Government and Regulation of the land and naval Forces;

To provide for calling forth the Militia to execute the Laws of the Union, suppress Insurrections and repel Invasions;

To provide for organizing, arming, and disciplining, the Militia, and for governing such Part of them as may be employed in the Service of the United States, reserving to the States respectively, the Appointment of the Officers, and the Authority of training the Militia according to the discipline prescribed by Congress;

To exercise exclusive Legislation in all Cases whatsoever, over such District (not exceeding ten Miles square) as may, by Cession of particular States, and the Acceptance of Congress, become the Seat of the Government of the United States, and to exercise like Authority over all Places purchased by the Consent of the Legislature of the State in which the Same shall be, for the Erection of Forts, Magazines, Arsenals, dock-Yards and other needful Buildings; And

To make all Laws which shall be necessary and proper for carrying into Execution the foregoing Powers, and all other Powers vested by this Constitution in the Government of the United States, or in any Department or Officer thereof.

Section 9: Powers Denied Congress.

The Migration or Importation of such Persons as any of the States now existing shall think proper to admit, shall not be prohibited by the Congress prior to the Year one thousand eight hundred and eight, but a Tax or duty may be imposed on such Importation, not exceeding ten dollars for each Person.

The Privilege of the Writ of Habeas Corpus shall not be suspended, unless when in Cases of Rebellion or Invasion the public Safety may require it.

No Bill of Attainder or ex post facto Law shall be passed.

No Capitation, or other direct, Tax shall be laid, unless in Proportion to the Census or Enumeration herein before directed to be taken.

No Tax or Duty shall be laid on Articles exported from any State.

No Preference shall be given by any Regulation of Commerce or Revenue to the Ports of one State over those of another: nor shall Vessels bound to, or from, one State, be obliged to enter, clear, or pay Duties in another.

No Money shall be drawn from the Treasury, but in Consequence of Appropriations made by Law; and a regular Statement and Account of the Receipts and Expenditures of all public Money shall be published from time to time.

No Title of Nobility shall be granted by the United States: And no Person holding any Office of Profit or Trust under them, shall, without the Consent of the Congress, accept of any present, Emolument, Office, or Title, of any kind whatever, from any King, Prince, or foreign State.

Section 10: Powers Denied to the States.

No State shall enter into any Treaty, Alliance, or Confederation; grant Letters of Marque and Reprisal; coin Money; emit Bills of Credit; make any Thing but gold and silver Coin a Tender in Payment of Debts; pass any Bill of Attainder, ex post facto Law, or Law impairing the Obligation of Contracts, or grant any Title of Nobility.

No State shall, without the Consent of the Congress, lay any Imposts or Duties on Imports or Exports, except what may be absolutely necessary for executing its inspection Laws: and the net Produce of all Duties and Imposts, laid by any State on Imports or Exports, shall be for the Use of the Treasury of the United States; and all such Laws shall be subject to the Revision and Control of the Congress.

No State shall, without the Consent of Congress, lay any Duty of

Tonnage, keep Troops, or Ships of War in time of Peace, enter into any Agreement or Compact with another State, or with a foreign Power, or engage in War, unless actually invaded, or in such imminent Danger as will not admit of delay.

Article II

Section 1

The executive Power shall be vested in a President of the United States of America.

He shall hold his Office during the Term of four Years, and, together with the Vice President, chosen for the same Term, be elected, as follows:

Each State shall appoint, in such Manner as the Legislature thereof may direct, a Number of Electors, equal to the whole Number of Senators and Representatives to which the State may be entitled in the Congress: but no Senator or Representative, or Person holding an Office of Trust or Profit under the United States, shall be appointed an Elector.

The Electors shall meet in their respective States, and vote by Ballot for two Persons, of whom one at least shall not be an Inhabitant of the same State with themselves. And they shall make a List of all the Persons voted for, and of the Number of Votes for each; which List they shall sign and certify, and transmit sealed to the Seat of the Government of the United States, directed to the President of the Senate. The President of the Senate shall, in the Presence of the Senate and House of Representatives, open all the Certificates, and the Votes shall then be counted. The Person having the greatest Number of Votes shall be the President, if such Number be a Majority of the whole Number of Electors appointed; and if there be more than one who have such Majority, and have an equal Number of Votes, then the House of Representatives shall immediately choose by Ballot one of them for President; and if no Person have a Majority, then from the five highest on the List the said House shall in like Manner choose the President. But in choosing the President, the Votes shall be taken by States, the Representation from each State having one Vote; A quorum for this Purpose shall consist of a Member or Members from two thirds of the States, and a Majority of all the States shall be necessary to a Choice.

In every Case, after the Choice of the President, the Person having the greatest Number of Votes of the Electors shall be the Vice President. But if there should remain two or more who have equal Votes, the Senate shall choose from them by Ballot the Vice President.

The Congress may determine the Time of choosing the Electors, and the Day on which they shall give their Votes; which Day shall be the same throughout the United States.

No Person except a natural-born Citizen, or a Citizen of the United States, at the time of the Adoption of this Constitution, shall be eligible to the Office of President; neither shall any person be eligible to that Office who shall not have attained to the Age of thirty-five Years, and been fourteen Years a Resident within the United States.

In Case of the Removal of the President from Office, or of his Death, Resignation, or Inability to discharge the Powers and Duties of the said Office, the Same shall devolve on the Vice President, and the Congress may by Law provide for the Case of Removal, Death, Resignation or Inability, both of the President and Vice President, declaring what Officer shall then act as President, and such Officer shall act accordingly, until the Disability be removed, or a President shall be elected.

The President shall, at stated Times, receive for his Services, a Compensation, which shall neither be increased nor diminished during the Period for which he shall have been elected, and he shall not receive within that Period any other Emolument from the United States, or any of them.

Before he enters on the Execution of his Office, he shall take the following Oath or Affirmation: "I do solemnly swear (or affirm) that I will faithfully execute the Office of President of the United States, and will to the best of my Ability, preserve, protect and defend the Constitution of the United States."

Section 2

The President shall be Commander in Chief of the Army and Navy of the United States, and of the Militia of the several States, when called into the actual Service of the United States; he may require the Opinion, in writing, of the principal Officer in each of the executive

Departments, upon any Subject relating to the Duties of their respective Offices, and he shall have Power to grant Reprieves and Pardons for Offenses against the United States, except in Cases of Impeachment.

He shall have Power, by and with the Advice and Consent of the Senate, to make Treaties, provided two thirds of the Senators present concur; and he shall nominate, and by and with the Advice and Consent of the Senate, shall appoint Ambassadors, other public Ministers and Consuls, Judges of the supreme Court, and all other Officers of the United States, whose Appointments are not herein otherwise provided for, and which shall be established by Law: but the Congress may by Law vest the Appointment of such inferior Officers, as they think proper, in the President alone, in the Courts of Law, or in the Heads of Departments.

The President shall have Power to fill up all Vacancies that may happen during the Recess of the Senate, by granting Commissions which shall expire at the End of their next Session.

Section 3

He shall from time to time give to the Congress Information of the State of the Union, and recommend to their Consideration such Measures as he shall judge necessary and expedient; he may, on extraordinary Occasions, convene both Houses, or either of them, and in Case of Disagreement between them, with Respect to the Time of Adjournment, he may adjourn them to such Time as he shall think proper; he shall receive Ambassadors and other public Ministers; he shall take Care that the Laws be faithfully executed, and shall Commission all the Officers of the United States.

Section 4:

The President, Vice President and all civil Officers of the United States, shall be removed from Office on Impeachment for, and Conviction of, Treason, Bribery, or other high Crimes and Misdemeanors.

Article III

Section 1

The judicial Power of the United States, shall be vested in one supreme Court, and in such inferior Courts as the Congress may from time to time ordain and establish. The Judges, both of the supreme and inferior Courts, shall hold their Offices during good Behavior, and shall, at stated Times, receive for their Services, a Compensation, which shall not be diminished during their Continuance in Office.

Section 2

The judicial Power shall extend to all Cases, in Law and Equity, arising under this Constitution, the Laws of the United States, and Treaties made, or which shall be made, under their Authority; to all Cases affecting Ambassadors, other public Ministers and Consuls; to all Cases of admiralty and maritime Jurisdiction; to Controversies to which the United States shall be a Party; to Controversies between two or more States; between a State and Citizens of another State; between Citizens of different States; between Citizens of the same State claiming Lands under Grants of different States, and between a State, or the Citizens thereof, and foreign States, Citizens or Subjects.

In all Cases affecting Ambassadors, other public Ministers and Consuls, and those in which a State shall be Party, the supreme Court shall have original Jurisdiction. In all the other Cases before mentioned, the supreme Court shall have appellate Jurisdiction, both as to Law and Fact, with such Exceptions, and under such Regulations as the Congress shall make.

The Trial of all Crimes, except in Cases of Impeachment; shall be by Jury; and such Trial shall be held in the State where the said Crimes shall have been committed; but when not committed within any State, the Trial shall be at such Place or Places as the Congress may by Law have directed.

Section 3

Treason against the United States, shall consist only in levying War against them, or in adhering to their Enemies, giving them Aid and Comfort. No Person shall be convicted of Treason unless on the Testimony of two Witnesses to the same overt Act, or on Confession in open Court.

The Congress shall have Power to declare the Punishment of Treason, but no Attainder of Treason shall work Corruption of Blood, or Forfeiture except during the Life of the Person attainted.

Article IV

Section 1

Full Faith and Credit shall be given in each State to the public Acts, Records, and judicial Proceedings of every other State. And the Congress may by general Laws prescribe the Manner in which such Acts, Records and Proceedings shall be proved, and the Effect thereof.

Section 2

The Citizens of each State shall be entitled to all Privileges and Immunities of Citizens in the several States.

A Person charged in any State with Treason, Felony, or other Crime, who shall flee from Justice, and be found in another State, shall on Demand of the executive Authority of the State from which he fled, be delivered up, to be removed to the State having Jurisdiction of the Crime.

No Person held to Service or Labor in one State, under the Laws thereof, escaping into another, shall, in Consequence of any Law or Regulation therein, be discharged from such Service or Labor, but shall be delivered up on Claim of the Party to whom such Service or Labor may be due.

Section 3

New States may be admitted by the Congress into this Union; but no new State shall be formed or erected within the Jurisdiction of any other State; nor any State be formed by the Junction of two or more States, or Parts of States, without the Consent of the Legislatures of the States concerned as well as of the Congress.

The Congress shall have Power to dispose of and make all needful Rules and Regulations respecting the Territory or other Property belonging to the United States; and nothing in this Constitution shall be so construed as to Prejudice any Claims of the United States, or of any particular State.

Section 4

The United States shall guarantee to every State in this Union a Republican Form of Government, and shall protect each of them against Invasion; and on Application of the Legislature, or of the Executive (when the Legislature cannot be convened) against domestic Violence.

Article V

The Congress, whenever two thirds of both Houses shall deem it necessary, shall propose Amendments to this Constitution, or, on the Application of the Legislatures of two thirds of the several States, shall call a Convention for proposing Amendments, which, in either Case, shall be valid to all Intents and Purposes, as Part of this Constitution, when ratified by the Legislatures of three fourths of the several States, or by Conventions in three fourths thereof, as the one or the other Mode of Ratification may be proposed by the Congress; Provided that no Amendment which may be made prior to the Year One thousand eight hundred and eight shall in any Manner affect the first and fourth Clauses in the Ninth Section of the first Article; and that no State, without its Consent, shall be deprived of its equal Suffrage in the Senate.

Article VI

All Debts contracted and Engagements entered into, before the Adoption of this Constitution, shall be as valid against the United States under this Constitution, as under the Confederation.

This Constitution and the Laws of the United States which shall be made in Pursuance thereof; and all Treaties made, or which shall be made, under the Authority of the United States, shall be the supreme Law of the Land; and the Judges in every State shall be bound thereby, any Thing in the Constitution or Laws of any State to the Contrary notwithstanding.

The Senators and Representatives before mentioned, and the Members of the several State Legislatures, and all executive and judicial Officers, both of the United States and of the several States, shall be bound by Oath or Affirmation, to support this Constitution; but no religious Test shall ever be required as a Qualification to any Office or public Trust under the United States.

Article VII

The Ratification of the Conventions of nine States, shall be sufficient for the Establishment of this Constitution between the States so ratifying the Same.

First Amendment

Congress shall make no law respecting an establishment of religion, or prohibiting the free exercise thereof; or abridging the freedom of speech, or of the press; or the right of the people peaceably to assemble, and to petition the Government for a redress of grievances.

Second Amendment

A well regulated Militia, being necessary to the security of a free State, the right of the people to keep and bear Arms, shall not be infringed.

Third Amendment

No Soldier shall, in time of peace be quartered in any house, without the consent of the Owner, nor in time of war, but in a manner to be prescribed by law.

Fourth Amendment

The right of the people to be secure in their persons, houses, papers, and effects, against unreasonable searches and seizures, shall not be violated, and no Warrants shall issue, but upon probable cause, supported by Oath or affirmation, and particularly describing the place to be searched, and the persons or things to be seized.

Fifth Amendment

No person shall be held to answer for a capital, or otherwise infamous crime, unless on a presentment of indictment of a Grand Jury, except in cases arising in the land or naval forces, or in the Militia, when in actual service in time of War or public danger; nor shall any person be subject for the same offense to be twice put in jeopardy of life or limb; nor shall be compelled in any criminal case to be a witness against himself, nor be deprived of life, liberty, or property, without due process of law; nor shall private property be taken for public use, without just compensation.

Sixth Amendment

In all criminal prosecutions, the accused shall enjoy the right to a speedy and public trial, by an impartial jury of the State and district wherein the crime shall have been committed, which district shall have been previously ascertained by law, and to be informed of the nature and cause of the accusation; to be confronted with the witnesses against him; to have compulsory process for obtaining witnesses in his favor, and to have the Assistance of Counsel for his defense.

Seventh Amendment

In Suits at common law, where the value in controversy shall exceed twenty dollars, the right of trial by jury shall be preserved, and no fact tried by a jury, shall be otherwise reexamined in any Court of the United States, than according to the rules of the common law.

Eighth Amendment

Excessive bail shall not be required, nor excessive fines imposed, nor cruel and unusual punishments inflicted.

Ninth Amendment

The enumeration in the Constitution, of certain rights, shall not be construed to deny or disparage others retained by the people.

10th Amendment

The powers not delegated to the United States by the Constitution, nor prohibited by it to the States, are reserved to the States respectively, or to the people.

11th Amendment

The Judicial power of the United States shall not be construed to extend to any suit in law or equity, commenced or prosecuted against one of the United States by Citizens of another State, or by Citizens or Subjects of any Foreign State.

12th Amendment

The Electors shall meet in their respective states and vote by ballot for President and Vice-President, one of whom, at least, shall not be an inhabitant of the same state with themselves; they shall name in their ballots the person voted for as President, and in distinct ballots the person voted for as Vice-President, and they shall make distinct lists of all persons voted for as President, and of all persons voted for as Vice-President, and of the number of votes for each, which lists they shall sign and certify, and transmit sealed to the seat of the government of the United States, directed to the President of the Senate.

The President of the Senate shall, in the presence of the Senate and House of Representatives, open all the certificates and the votes shall then be counted. The person having the greatest number of votes for President, shall be the President, if such number be a majority of the whole number of Electors appointed; and if no person have such majority, then from the persons having the highest numbers not exceeding three on the list of those voted for as President, the House of Representatives shall choose immediately, by ballot, the President. But in choosing the President, the votes shall be taken by states, the representation from each state having one vote; a quorum for this purpose shall consist of a member or members from two-thirds of the states, and a majority of all the states shall be necessary to a choice. And if the House of Representatives shall not choose a President whenever the right of choice shall devolve upon them, before the fourth day of March next following, then the Vice-President shall act as President, as in case of the death or other constitutional disability of the President.

The person having the greatest number of votes as Vice-President, shall be the Vice-President, if such number be a majority of the whole number of Electors appointed, and if no person have a majority, then from the two highest numbers on the list, the Senate shall choose the Vice-President; a quorum for the purpose shall consist of two-thirds of the whole number of Senators, and a majority of the whole number shall be necessary to a choice. But no person constitutionally ineligible to the office of President shall be eligible to that of Vice-President of the United States.

13th Amendment

Section 1

Neither slavery nor involuntary servitude, except as a punishment for crime whereof the party shall have been duly convicted, shall exist within the United States, or any place subject to their jurisdiction.

Section 2

Congress shall have power to enforce this article by appropriate legislation.

14th Amendment

Section 1

All persons born or naturalized in the United States, and subject to the jurisdiction thereof, are citizens of the United States and of the State wherein they reside. No State shall make or enforce any law which shall abridge the privileges or immunities of citizens of the United States; nor shall any State deprive any person of life, liberty, or property, without due process of law; nor deny to any person within its jurisdiction the equal protection of the laws.

Section 2

Representatives shall be apportioned among the several States according to their respective numbers, counting the whole number of persons in each State, excluding Indians not taxed. But when the right to vote at any election for the choice of electors for President and Vice-President of the United States, Representatives in Congress, the Executive and Judicial officers of a State, or the members of the Legislature thereof, is denied to any of the male inhabitants of such State, being twenty-one years of age, and citizens of the United States, or in any way abridged, except for participation in rebellion, or other crime, the basis of representation therein shall be reduced in the proportion which the number of such male citizens shall bear to the whole number of male citizens twenty-one years of age in such State.

Section 3

No person shall be a Senator or Representative in Congress, or elector of President and Vice-President, or hold any office, civil or military, under the United States, or under any State, who, having previously taken an oath, as a member of Congress, or as an officer of the United States, or as a member of any State legislature, or as an executive or judicial officer of any State, to support the Constitution of the United States, shall have engaged in insurrection or rebellion against the same, or given aid or comfort to the enemies thereof. But Congress may by a vote of two-thirds of each House, remove such disability.

Section 4

The validity of the public debt of the United States, authorized by law, including debts incurred for payment of pensions and bounties for services in suppressing insurrection or rebellion, shall not be questioned. But neither the United States nor any State shall assume or pay any debt or obligation incurred in aid of insurrection or rebellion against the United States, or any claim for the loss or emancipation of any slave; but all such debts, obligations and claims shall be held illegal and void.

Section 5

The Congress shall have the power to enforce, by appropriate legislation, the provisions of this article.

15th Amendment

Section 1

The right of citizens of the United States to vote shall not be denied or abridged by the United States or by any State on account of race, color, or previous condition of servitude.

Section 2

The Congress shall have the power to enforce this article by appropriate legislation.

16th Amendment

The Congress shall have power to lay and collect taxes on incomes, from whatever source derived, without apportionment among the several States, and without regard to any census or enumeration.

17th Amendment

The Senate of the United States shall be composed of two Senators from each State, elected by the people thereof, for six years; and each Senator shall have one vote. The electors in each State shall have the qualifications requisite for electors of the most numerous branch of the State legislatures.

When vacancies happen in the representation of any State in the Senate, the executive authority of such State shall issue writs of election to fill such vacancies: **Provided**, That the legislature of any State may empower the executive thereof to make temporary appointments until the people fill the vacancies by election as the legislature may direct.

This amendment shall not be so construed as to affect the election or term of any Senator chosen before it becomes valid as part of the Constitution.

18th Amendment

Section 1

After one year from the ratification of this article the manufacture, sale, or transportation of intoxicating liquors within, the importation thereof into, or the exportation thereof from the United States and all territory subject to the jurisdiction thereof for beverage purposes is hereby prohibited.

Section 2

The Congress and the several States shall have concurrent power to enforce this article by appropriate legislation.

Section 3

This article shall be inoperative unless it shall have been ratified as an amendment to the Constitution by the legislatures of the several States, as provided in the Constitution, within seven years from the date of the submission hereof to the States by the Congress.

19th Amendment

Section 1

The right of citizens of the United States to vote shall not be denied or abridged by the United States or by any State on account of sex.

Section 2

Congress shall have power to enforce this article by appropriate legislation.

20th Amendment

Section 1

The terms of the President and the Vice President shall end at noon on the 20th day of January, and the terms of Senators and Representatives at noon on the 3d day of January, of the years in which such terms would have ended if this article had not been ratified; and the terms of their successors shall then begin.

Section 2

The Congress shall assemble at least once in every year, and such meeting shall begin at noon on the 3d day of January, unless they shall by law appoint a different day.

Section 3

If, at the time fixed for the beginning of the term of the President, the President-elect shall have died, the Vice President-elect shall become President. If a President shall not have been chosen before the time fixed for the beginning of his term, or if the President-elect shall have failed to qualify, then the Vice President-elect shall act as President until a President shall have qualified; and the Congress may by law provide for the case wherein neither a President-elect nor a Vice President shall have qualified, declaring who shall then act as President, or the manner in which one who is to act shall be selected, and such person shall act accordingly until a President or Vice President shall have qualified.

Section 4

The Congress may by law provide for the case of the death of any of the persons from whom the House of Representatives may choose a President whenever the right of choice shall have devolved upon them, and for the case of the death of any of the persons from whom the Senate may choose a Vice President whenever the right of choice shall have devolved upon them.

Section 5

Sections 1 and 2 shall take effect on the 15th day of October following the ratification of this article.

Section 6

This article shall be inoperative unless it shall have been ratified as an amendment to the Constitution by the legislatures of three-fourths of the several States within seven years from the date of its submission.

21st Amendment

Section 1

The eighteenth article of amendment to the Constitution of the United States is hereby repealed.

Section 2

The transportation or importation into any State, Territory, or Possession of the United States for delivery or use therein of intoxicating liquors, in violation of the laws thereof, is hereby prohibited.

Section 3

This article shall be inoperative unless it shall have been ratified as an amendment to the Constitution by conventions in the several States, as provided in the Constitution, within seven years from the date of the submission hereof to the States by the Congress.

22nd Amendment

Section 1

No person shall be elected to the office of the President more than twice, and no person who has held the office of President, or acted as President, for more than two years of a term to which some other person was elected President shall be elected to the office of President more than once. But this Article shall not apply to any person holding the office of President when this Article was proposed by Congress, and shall not prevent any person who may be holding the office of President, or acting as President, during the term within which this Article becomes operative from holding the office of President or acting as President during the remainder of such term.

Section 2

This article shall be inoperative unless it shall have been ratified as an amendment to the Constitution by the legislatures of three-fourths of the several States within seven years from the date of its submission to the States by the Congress.

23rd Amendment

Section 1

The District constituting the seat of Government of the United States shall appoint in such manner as Congress may direct: A number of electors of President and Vice President equal to the whole number of Senators and Representatives in Congress to which the District would be entitled if it were a State, but in no event more than the least populous State; they shall be in addition to those appointed by the States, but they shall be considered, for the purposes of the election of President and Vice President, to be electors appointed by a State; and they shall meet in the District and perform such duties as provided by the twelfth article of amendment.

Section 2

The Congress shall have power to enforce this article by appropriate legislation.

24th Amendment

Section 1

The right of citizens of the United States to vote in any primary or other election for President or Vice President, for electors for President or Vice President, or for Senator or Representative in Congress, shall not be denied or abridged by the United States or any State by reason of failure to pay poll tax or other tax.

Section 2

The Congress shall have power to enforce this article by appropriate legislation.

25th Amendment

Section 1

In case of the removal of the President from office or of his death or resignation, the Vice President shall become President.

Section 2

Whenever there is a vacancy in the office of the Vice President, the President shall nominate a Vice President who shall take office upon confirmation by a majority vote of both Houses of Congress.

Section 3

Whenever the President transmits to the President pro tempore of the Senate and the Speaker of the House of Representatives his written declaration that he is unable to discharge the powers and duties of his office, and until he transmits to them a written declaration to the contrary, such powers and duties shall be discharged by the Vice President as Acting President.

Section 4

Whenever the Vice President and a majority of either the principal officers of the executive departments or of such other body as Congress may by law provide, transmit to the President pro tempore of the Senate and the Speaker of the House of Representatives their written declaration that the President is unable to discharge the powers and duties of his office, the Vice President shall immediately assume the powers and duties of the office as Acting President.

Thereafter, when the President transmits to the President pro tempore of the Senate and the Speaker of the House of Representatives his written declaration that no inability exists, he shall resume the powers and duties of his office unless the Vice President and a majority of either the principal officers of the executive department or of such other body as Congress may by law provide, transmit within four days to the President pro tempore of the Senate and the Speaker of the House of Representatives their written declaration that the President is unable to discharge the powers and duties of his office. Thereupon Congress shall decide the issue, assembling within forty-eight hours for that purpose if not in session. If the Congress, within twenty-one days after receipt of the latter written declaration, or, if Congress is not in session, within twenty-one days after Congress is required to assemble, determines by two-thirds vote of both Houses that the President is unable to discharge the powers and duties of his office, the Vice President shall continue to discharge the same as Acting President; otherwise, the President shall resume the powers and duties of his office.

26th Amendment

Section 1

The right of citizens of the United States, who are eighteen years of age or older, to vote shall not be denied or abridged by the United States or by any State on account of age.

Section 2

The Congress shall have power to enforce this article by appropriate legislation.

27th Amendment

No law, varying the compensation for the services of the Senators and Representatives, shall take effect, until an election of representatives shall have intervened.

APPENDIX II: Gerrymandering and Voter Suppression Efforts

Small State Bias in Constitution

Even before the constitution, the country was divided into two populations, rural and urban, that differed in perspective and values. The great compromise, which allocated two senate seats to each of the thirteen initial states regardless of size, was necessary to gain agreement for the union.

This compromise resulted in a built-in advantage to smaller, more rural states to make sure they would not be subject to a "tyranny of the majority."

The electoral college to select the President, which allocates votes based upon the total number of seats a state has (both House and Senate) carries this advantage into presidential elections.

This built-in bias was viewed as a necessary "countervailing" weight against the larger, urban states.

However, the founding fathers did not anticipate the possibility of a "tyranny of the minority," where smaller states would consistently thwart the will of the majority—the predicament we appear to be in now.

The built-in bias of the constitution to the rural, less populated states has been extended by systematic measures to increase rural representation in congress and to thwart many of those groups who live in, or sympathize with, urban populations—minorities, elderly, disabled, and newly minted citizens.

Origins of Gerrymdandering

The Constitution requires a census of the US population every 10 years and Congressional House seats and Congressional districts are adjusted to maintain the same number of total House seats (435) in congress. If states gain population, they gain seats; if they lose population, they lose seats. At the same time, state house and senate seats, which are all apportioned by district, are also reviewed and may be re-drawn.

Within each state, factions tend to congregate in specific geographic regions; the urbanites in concentrated areas of commerce and the rural population in thinly populated agricultural areas. Location of residence makes no difference when statewide elections take place, but when representation is calculated for geographic districts, then residency can make a big difference because district boundaries can be changed to skew representation to either rural or urban populations for both federal and state seats. This skewing is called Gerrymandering.

Elbridge Gerry was a Founding Father and the fifth Vice President of the United States, serving under James Madison. He was the governor of Massachusetts from 1810 to 1812. While he was governor, Gerry made the connection that, given that people of similar interests tended to live in the same areas, he could draw district boundaries for senate seats in Massachusetts to give his party an advantage. One of the senate districts that he devised was so convoluted and sprawling that it looked like a salamander. This shape was known as Gerry's Salamander, and eventually the two terms were consolidated into "Gerrymander."

How Gerrymandering Works

To see how Gerrymandering works, consider Table A1. This community has 12 citizens, six Republicans in black, and six Democrats in gray. Republicans live in the first two columns and the first three rows. Democrats live in the remaining areas.

Assume we have 4 districts for the state house. Given that we have an equal number of Republicans and Democrats, we expect on average to have two Republican seats and two Democratic seats if the districts are fairly apportioned. This is shown in the Fair Districts graph.

However, the four district boundaries can be re-drawn so that, in the first case, three Republican seats and one Democratic seat on average will be selected for the House. There is also another geographic configuration of district boundaries so that three Democratic seats and one Republican seat will be selected.

Notice that populations do not have to relocate; merely by re-drawing district boundaries, the number of seats for a particular party can be

Table A1: GERRYMANDERING

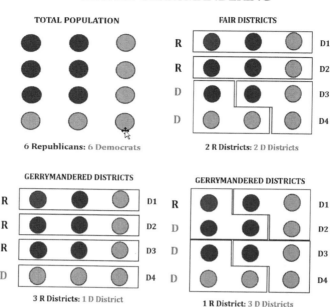

increased.

A Solution to Gerrymandering

The best solution to Gerrymandering is to require each state to set up an independent, bi-partisan commission that will develop an algorithm to apportion seats without regard to the registration status of voters. Several such algorithms have been demonstrated.

Voter Suppression Techniques

Because many minorities, disabled, and poor vote Democratic, the Republican Party aggressively tries to limit them from voting. A quick search of ChatGPT provides the following list of voter suppression techniques being employed by the Republican Party in areas they control. This is an incomplete list; development of suppression techniques is limited only by the perpetrator's imagination.

1. **Gerrymandering Electoral Districts to Favor the Republican Party:** Manipulating the boundaries of electoral districts to create a political advantage for Republicans. (Source: Washington Post.)

2. **Fake Registration Sites:** Elon Musk's PAC has set up a website to collect registration information, but data are not being sent to the states' Boards of Election. (Source: https://tinyurl.com/FakeRegistration.)

3. **Strict Voter ID Requirements:** Laws that require voters to present specific forms of photo identification at the polls, which can disproportionately affect minorities, the elderly, and low-income voters who are less likely to possess such IDs. (Source: Brennan Center for Justice.)

4. **Voter Roll Purges:** The process of removing inactive voters from the voter registration lists. This can lead to eligible voters being incorrectly removed. (Source: Reuters.)

5. **Closing or Reducing Polling Locations:** Often occurs in areas with higher populations of minority voters, leading to long lines and longer travel times to vote. (Source: Leadership Conference on Civil and Human Rights.)

6. **Limiting Early Voting Days and Hours:** Reducing the number of days and hours available for early voting, which can disproportionately impact those who cannot take time off work on Election Day. (Source: American Civil Liberties Union (ACLU).)

7. **Intimidation Tactics at Polls:** This includes tactics such as placing law enforcement at polling places, aggressive questioning of voters, or distributing misleading information about voting requirements. (Source: USA Today.)

8. **Imposing Barriers on Absentee and Mail-in Voting:** Implementing strict requirements for requesting, completing, and returning absentee ballots, such as requiring notarized signatures or limiting drop-off locations. (Source: NPR.)

9. **Restricting Voting Rights for Former Felons:** Laws that prevent people with felony convictions from voting, even after they have served their sentences. These laws disproportionately affect African Americans. (Source: Sentencing Project.)

10. **Requiring Voter Registration Information to Exactly Match Other Records:** Small discrepancies, such as a missing hyphen or middle initial, can lead to voter registrations being rejected. (Source: ACLU.)

11. **Spreading False Information About Voting Procedures:** Disseminating incorrect information about how, when, and where to vote, often targeting minority communities. (Source: The Guardian.)

12. **Using Caging Lists:** This involves sending mail to registered voters and challenging the registration of those whose mail is returned undelivered. This can disproportionately affect minority and low-income voters who may have unstable housing situations. (Source: Brennan Center for Justice.)

13. **Frequent Relocation of Polling Places:** Moving polling locations frequently and without adequate notice, making it difficult for voters, particularly those without reliable transportation, to find and access their polling place. (Source: New York Times.)

14. **Insufficient Language Assistance:** Failing to provide adequate language assistance and translated materials for non-English-speaking voters, in violation of the Voting Rights Act. (Source: American Civil Liberties Union (ACLU).)

15. **Aggressive Challenges to Voter Eligibility:** Stationing poll watchers to challenge the eligibility of voters at polling places, often targeting minority communities. (Source: The Atlantic.)

16. **Restricting Voter Registration Drives:** Implementing laws or policies that make it more difficult for organizations to conduct voter registration drives, which are critical for registering minority and low-income voters. (Source: Brennan Center for Justice.)

17. **Criminalizing Minor Mistakes:** Laws that penalize voters for minor errors on registration forms or ballots, which can disproportionately affect new voters, minorities, and the elderly. (Source: The Guardian.)

18. **Limiting Access to Absentee Ballots:** Imposing restrictive rules for obtaining and submitting absentee ballots, such as requiring voters to provide a valid excuse, limiting who can return a ballot on behalf of a voter, or rejecting ballots for minor errors. (Source:

National Public Radio (NPR).)

19. **Proof of Citizenship:** Requiring documentary proof of citizenship to register to vote, which can be a barrier for many eligible voters. (Source: Brennan Center for Justice.)

############

Why I am a Democrat. *Jim Veney, Professor Emeritus UNC-Chapel Hill.*

"While I agree (or don't disagree) with some of the goals of the Republican party, there is one overarching reason that I will always vote Democrat and will never vote Republican. This is the reason:

The entire world is divided into two groups. Those two groups are the We's and the They's. It's easy enough to understand that the We's are always good and right and the They's are always bad and wrong. In simple terms, We good, They bad.

Many of the World's problems might go away if we could increase the number of people in the We group and decrease the number of people in the They group. It's my lifetime observation that Democrats are mostly working to increase the size of the We group, while Republicans are mostly working to increase the size of the They group. For this single reason alone, I cannot support a Republican candidate for any office."

APPENDIX III: Oaths to the Constitution

Service Oaths

"The Senators and Representatives before mentioned, and the Members of the several State Legislatures, and all executive and judicial Officers, both of the United States and of the several States, shall be bound by Oath or Affirmation, to support this Constitution; but no religious Test shall ever be required as a Qualification to any Office or public Trust under the United States." US Constitution.

The President of the United States takes the following oath as required by Article 2, Section 1 of the Constitution:

> I do solemnly swear (or affirm) that I will faithfully execute the Office of President of the United States, and will to the best of my ability, preserve, protect and defend the Constitution of the United States.

All elected officials take the following oath when sworn into office:

> I, (Name) do solemnly swear (or affirm) that I will support and defend the Constitution of the United States against all enemies, foreign and domestic; that I will bear true faith and allegiance to the same; that I take this obligation freely, without any mental reservation or purpose of evasion; and that I will well and faithfully discharge the duties of the office on which I am about to enter. So help me God.

All enlisted personal in the US Military take the following oath:

> I, (Name) do solemnly swear (or affirm) that I will support and defend the Constitution of the United States against all enemies, foreign and domestic; that I will bear true faith and allegiance to the same; and that I will obey the orders of the President of the United States and the orders of the

officers appointed over me, according to regulations and the Uniform Code of Military Justice. So help me God.

All officers in the US Military take the following oath:

> I, (Name), having been appointed an officer in the (Military Branch) of the United States, as indicated above in the grade of (Rank) do solemnly swear (or affirm) that I will support and defend the Constitution of the United States against all enemies, foreign or domestic, that I will bear true faith and allegiance to the same; that I take this obligation freely, without any mental reservation or purpose of evasion; and that I will well and faithfully discharge the duties of the office upon which I am about to enter. So help me God.

A Candidate's Oath

If we require elected officials to swear an oath to the Constitution, we should also require every candidate who runs for office to swear an oath to the Constitution, the rule of law, and non-violence in our elections. Here is one such Candidate's Oath.

- I believe that true democracy requires everyone's voice and vote and will do everything in my power to make that possible.
- I believe in, and will abide by, provisions of the American Constitution as interpreted by the US judicial system.
- I believe that transparency, truth, honesty, and openness in all public discourse are essential and will do nothing to undermine them.
- I believe in, and will follow, the Rule of Law in all civil, criminal, and political disagreements and proceedings.
- I believe that free and fair elections are the foundation of a civilized nation and will not needlessly contest their outcome or sow doubt about their validity.
- I believe that violence is counter-productive to a civilized society and will do all in my power to prevent it and I will use extreme caution in using it to carry out my duties.
- I believe that checks and balances throughout government are essential to restrain our worst impulses and lead to better outcomes

for the nation.

- I believe we are stronger when everyone's interests are considered and will balance the needs of the many against the interest of the few. I will not place my interests ahead of others because I serve the people in my community.
- I will resist authoritarianism in all its forms and will fight attempts, foreign and domestic, to undermine our democracy.
- To all these beliefs I swear to remain faithful. So help me God.

As citizens, we should commit to voting only for those candidates, Democrat, Republican, or Other who will take the Candidate's Oath.

Society for the Rule of Law

The Society for the Rule of Law is a conservative organization that asks citizens to commit to the fundamental principles of our constitutional democracy and to repudiate MAGA attempts to overthrow it. This pledge is fundamental to the American polity and the common ground upon which conservatives and liberals; Real Republicans, Democrats, Libertarians and the Green Party may debate, decide and agree upon actions for the public good without violence. It is defining framework of American governance and stands in stark contrast to the authoritarian framework of MAGA Republicans.

Whereas America is a "nation of laws, not of men."

Whereas the Constitution of the United States and the rule of law provide for and guarantee that "we the people" possess and shall exercise the powers of self-government through the free and fair elections of our representatives.

Whereas citizens of the United States of America have a duty to preserve, protect, and defend the Constitution of the United States and the rule of law.

Whereas the Constitution's separation of powers provides that the Congress, the Executive, and the Judiciary each serves as a check and balance on the other two branches of government.

Whereas the independence of the Supreme Court and the

Federal Judiciary is essential to constitutional government and the rule of law.

Whereas our government shall uphold the ideals of equality under the law and equal justice for all.

Be It Resolved that American citizens have a duty:

To accept the legitimacy, respect the authority, and abide by the decisions and judgments of the federal courts interpreting the Constitution and laws of the United States.

To respect the rule of law by honoring the truth and speaking against untruths that undermine respect for the Constitution, the rule of law, and the courts of the United States.

To oppose any and all efforts by false accusation, threat, or similarly to undermine respect for the federal courts and the individual justices and judges who serve on the courts of the United States.

To support and defend the fundamental American principle that no person is above, beneath, or beyond the law.

To respect, support, and defend the constitutional rights of all Americans.

To accept, honor, and respect the results of elections by the American people.

To respect, support, and insist upon the peaceful transfer of power upon which our constitutional republic is premised and depends.

To respect, support, and defend the right of aggrieved candidates to invoke the judicial process to challenge the results of elections and the corresponding obligation of such candidates to respect the resulting decisions of the courts of law.

To hold government officials, political leaders, candidates for high office, and leaders of the political parties responsible and accountable for the preservation, protection, and defense of the Constitution and the rule of law, and for adherence to the constitutional principles of America's great experiment in democracy and constitutional self-government.

To affirm and reaffirm that the duty and responsibility of government and governmental officials is to the Constitution, the rule of law, and to the American people, and that it is the duty and responsibility of all public officials to serve all citizens, irrespective of their political party or other affiliation, association, or identity.

To honor America by preserving, protecting, and defending the Constitution of the United States, the rule of law, and America's democracy.

Society for The Rule of Law

When dictators seek to destroy the freedoms of men, their first target is the legal profession and through it the rule of law. Leon Jaworski

RAW Guardians

Firefighters, Law Enforcement and the military are special citizens in our Constitutional Democracy; they are the guardians of our society and protectors of American citizens. They swear oaths of allegiance to the Constitution of the United States and pledge that they "will well and faithfully discharge the duties upon which they are about to enter." Unfortunately, a few have broken their oaths and joined MAGA organizations that want to destroy our constitutional form of government. These oath-breakers may be found in many far right groups advocating violent overthrow of the government. They are actively planning to become Donald Trump's personal militia.

I invite all active and retired Responders and Warriors (RAW) to repudiate these oath-breakers and reaffirm their commitment to the Constitution and for the principles it stands for. The following website will allow RAW Guardians to publically reaffirm their commitment.

More Info   Raw Guardians

American Women Fighting for Democracy

American Men Fighting for Democracy

* * *

BIOGRAPHY

Jim Porto is a lifelong Democrat, first voting in 1968. He holds a Ph.D. in Public Policy from UNC-Chapel Hill, a Master of Public Administration from N.C. State University and a Baccalaureate in Psychology from Duke University. He taught at UNC-Chapel hill for almost 30 years before retiring.

He served in Vietnam as a Marine Helicopter pilot and was promoted to the rank of LtCol in the UMSC reserve. He is a former mayor of the Town of Carrboro, NC.

He is a past Committee Member, Debt Affordability Advisory Committee (2005-2013) in N.C., appointed by Speaker of the House and past Board Member, N.C. Capital Facilities Financing Agency (2001-2004), also appointed by Speaker of the House.

He volunteers in his local precinct and is currently serving as the Chair of Townhall Precinct for the Democratic Party in Carrboro, N.C.

Contact information: jvporto2@gmail.com

Made in the USA
Middletown, DE
19 September 2024